# THE ZEN OF ZIM

ALSO BY DON ZIMMER
WITH BILL MADDEN

*Zim—A Baseball Life*

# DON ZIMMER

## WITH BILL MADDEN

### FOREWORD BY LOU PINIELLA

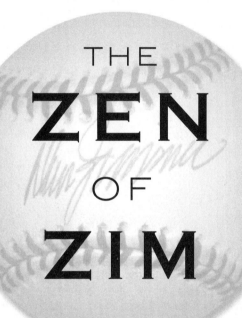

THE
**ZEN**
OF
**ZIM**

## Baseballs, Beanballs, and Bosses

THOMAS DUNNE BOOKS
ST. MARTIN'S PRESS NEW YORK

This book is dedicated to Tom Zimmer, Donna Zimmer Mollica, Steven Madden, and Thomas Madden, the authors' children, all of whom grew up in the baseball life and have made us forever proud by how they've lived their own lives.

It is also dedicated to the hundreds of mutual friends, past and present, the authors have made in baseball— players, managers, coaches, scouts, executives, umpires, broadcasters, and sportswriters. You all know who you are.

THOMAS DUNNE BOOKS.
An imprint of St. Martin's Press.

www.stmartins.com

Design by Kathryn Parise

ISBN 0-312-33430-3
EAN 978-0312-33430-7

First Edition: June 2004

10  9  8  7  6  5  4  3  2  1

# CONTENTS

# Contents

# ACKNOWLEDGMENTS

**T**he authors gratefully acknowledge the following people for their assistance on this book:

Soot Zimmer, whose scrapbooks and photo collection of her husband's career were invaluable.

Lillian Madden, whose scrupulous proofreading of this book (after all the previous ones) may have finally now elevated her to "student of the game" status.

Neil Leifer, photographer extraordinaire, whose artistry with the lens is exemplified on the cover of this book. A friend, colleague, and "good luck charm" on all the Madden book projects, he did what he could with the subject in the author photo.

Bill Francis of the National Baseball Hall of Fame and Museum library, who was tireless in his research of facts and events chronicled by Mr. Zimmer.

Jeff Idelson, vice president of communications of the National Baseball Hall of Fame and Museum, who extended the authors all the courtesies of the Hall.

Jack Lang, newspaperman emeritus and the last surviving Brooklyn Dodgers "beat man," who provided numerous supporting anecdotes, facts, and information for the 1955 Dodgers chapter.

Scotty Browne, Jimmy Converso, Pete Edelman, Dawn Jackson, Ellen Locker, Scott Widener, Shirley Wong, and Faigi Rosenthal of the New York *Daily News* library, who gave of their time to dig through the archives in providing supporting research material.

The Elias Sports Bureau, especially Seymour Siwoff, Bob Rosen, and Tom Hirdt, who researched many of the statistics to which Mr. Zimmer refers, especially those in the 1955 Dodgers chapter.

Eric Meskauskas, New York *Daily News* photo editor, who aided in the discovery and acquisition of some of the photos contained in the centerfold.

Art Berke, vice president of communications for *Sports Illustrated*, a pal for life who, as always, cheerfully made available the *SI* archives for research.

Elaine Kauffman, wise counsel to writers, who nurtures and scolds but always supports.

John Parsley, who had the yeoman task of coordinating all the elements—text, editing corrections, inserts, photos—of this book for Thomas Dunne Books.

Arun Kristian Das, for his painstaking copyediting of this project.

Mark Steven Long, St. Martin's production editor, who put everything together.

Pete Wolverton, Thomas Dunne Books editor, who believed in this project from the get-go and then made it happen.

Rob Wilson, agent, confidant, and valued friend, whose support and belief have been a continued inspiration.

# FOREWORD

BY LOU PINIELLA

After my first season as manager of the Tampa Bay Devil Rays ended in 2003, I felt I needed a vacation. It had been a tough year, losing 99 games as we did, and even though we were competitive in just about all of them, I thought it would be nice for my wife and I to get a break from baseball, so we decided to take a trip to Spain and Italy that October. We'd been on the trip for nearly two weeks, totally removed from baseball, when one day I happened to be sitting in a cafe in Venice, where there was a TV screen up on the wall tuned to CNN.

As I was sitting there having a drink with my friend Tony Gonzalez, I was periodically glancing up at the TV when my attention was suddenly drawn by footage of a baseball melee between the Yankees and the Red Sox. I realized this was the American League Championship Series and as I thought to myself, "Old rivalries sure die hard," I did a double-take at the sight of my old pal Don Zimmer running across the field and charging Pedro Martinez. As Zim threw this haymaker and Pedro proceeded to toss him to the ground, I burst into laughter. "Tony," I yelled, "I can't believe what I'm seeing here! I need another martini!" I thought I was watching another bullfight in Spain!

I know Don regrets that the incident ever happened, but you know what? This is a man with passion. Passion for the game, passion for his friends, teammates, and family, passion for everything he does. To me, Don Zimmer is a baseball treasure and I'm glad to have him on my staff.

I first got to know Don in the late '70s, when he was managing the Red Sox and I was playing for the Yankees. Whenever our two teams met, I'd invariably wind up talking baseball and horse racing with Don around the batting cage. Unfortunately, I once made the mistake of talking too much to him when I offhandedly mentioned to him that the one pitcher whose pitches I couldn't pick up was his reliever, Bill Campbell. After that, it seemed every time I came to the plate from the seventh inning on against Boston, here came Zimmer to the mound, summoning in Bill Campbell.

Later, when I became manager of the Yankees, I hired Don as a coach for half a season. After that, we both went our separate ways, but it was easy for me to keep track of him. He always seemed to be in the middle of things—like that brawl with the Red Sox—and I was keenly aware of how valuable his presence was to Joe Torre during the Yankees' string of championships from 1996 to 2003. When Don left the Yankees after the 2003 season, he made it clear he wasn't retiring unless nobody offered him a job.

But here's what I think: Guys like Don Zimmer, who have been around the game for more than fifty years, shouldn't have to take the uniform off until they want to. Don's an old dinosaur and he's a joy to be around. He's a character and baseball needs characters. Much more than that, though, he's a man with a half century of baseball knowledge who knows how to communicate it to the young kids today. I call him a nice natural resource. It would have been foolish for us not to avail ourselves of his expertise.

I know I was glad he'd made himself available, even though we didn't have any vacancies on our coaching staff in Tampa Bay. We hired Don for his knowledge and his experience, and we gave him the title "senior advisor." I never told him this, but I really hired him as a bodyguard.

# PROLOGUE

**Yankee Stadium,**

**October 26, 2003,**

**12:07 P.M.**

I t was really over now, all of it. Josh Beckett, the precocious twenty-three-year-old right-hander for the Florida Marlins had just completed his 5-hit, 9 strikeout, 2–0 masterpiece over the New York Yankees in the sixth game of the World Series to put a stunning climax to the 2003 baseball season. Unlike two years earlier, when the Joe Torre Yankees had tasted unaccustomed defeat in the World Series to the Arizona Diamondbacks, Don Zimmer did not bother to linger in the dugout to watch the new champions celebrate on the field. He'd been preparing for this moment for months, rehearsed his farewell speech over and over, and then, a week earlier, after the Yankees defeated the Boston Red Sox in the most physically, mentally, and emotionally draining series he'd ever been a part of in his fifty-five years in baseball, he'd been unable to contain himself when a reporter confronted him in the coaches' room and asked him how much this win had meant to him.

"All I can say is, this is one asshole he won't have to worry about firing," he blurted to the startled reporter, " 'cause I won't be back. I'm a human being and I ain't been treated like one in eleven months."

He had made up his mind months earlier that this would be his final season as Torre's bench coach and sidekick. Nearly a year of continual, humiliating slights by the Yankees owner, George Steinbrenner, a man who'd been his friend for more than twenty-five years, had brought him to this. He never knew what he possibly could have done to deserve this sort of shabby treatment from a boss who'd savored the spoils of six pennants and four world championships in his eight years there, but by this time he no longer cared. He would have his say, speak his piece about Steinbrenner, and be out of there. He'd even told a couple of longtime baseball reporters whom he considered friends to wait outside the coaches' room whenever the World Series ended, and he'd elaborate on the bitterness he'd been unable to keep inside himself a week earlier.

But in the meantime, his wife, Soot, the pillar of calm and stability in his life for fifty-two years and the one person who could ever get him to see the value of reason and restraint at times like this, had gently admonished him. "I know how you feel about the man," she had said, "and you have every right to feel that way. But you shouldn't hold a press conference after the World Series to say what you feel. It'll just make you look like a little man."

There were tears in her eyes as she spoke to him, something he had rarely seen throughout all the baseball tumult they had shared over six major league decades from Brooklyn to Los Angeles, Cincinnati, Washington, San Diego, Dallas, Boston, Chicago, Denver, and finally back to New York. They were the tears of a woman who also hated seeing this apparently last and most rewarding chapter of his baseball life come to an end like this, all because her man had been wounded like never before.

So now here he was, slowly removing his Yankee pinstripes for the last time, and in this moment of solitude, the anger within him had somehow begun to subside. Instead, he found his mind wandering, suddenly consumed with sweet memories of a renewed love story with New York, tinged no less by the sadness of a friendship smashed for no reason.

He thought of Paul O'Neill, absent this past year save for occasional appearances as a part-time broadcaster with the team's YES Network, and he smiled at the memory of all those temper tantrums, which only he could defuse with a simple grin. "What's so funny?" O'Neill would bark, tossing his bat in anger after being rung up on a pitch only he had deemed out of the strike zone. "You are," Zimmer would shoot back.

He'd always felt a kinship with O'Neill since they shared the same hometown, Cincinnati, and he felt a similar bond with Joe Girardi, with whom he'd shared ten seasons in the majors in three mutual stopovers on the major league highway: Wrigley Field in Chicago, Colorado, and finally in New York for three world championship runs. At the thought of Girardi, however, he felt a flash of renewed anger over the impassioned arguments he'd had with Steinbrenner about the catcher's worth. He'd loved Girardi's grit and selflessness, and he wondered if their paths might cross one more time, presumably when Girardi would be managing somewhere. "All he ever did was win," Zimmer thought.

The team he'd known—the one that had been as special as any he'd ever been around—was now in large part scattered by the winds of time. O'Neill, Brosius, Big Daddy, Sojo, Boggsie, Wetteland, Knoblauch, even Darryl, all retired; the others, Girardi, Tino, Stanton, El Duque, summarily discarded to play out their careers elsewhere. It is the way of life in professional sports—players get old, teams change, life evolves—and he understood this more than anyone. The memories of the warm times and the glories they shared were what last forever, and nothing and no one could ever diminish any of that for him.

And then there were the ones still here, in the big room around the corner from his—Jeter, Bernie, Rivera, Pettitte, Rocket, Posada; and his comrades-in-arms on the coaching staff, Mel, Willie, Maz, Monteleone, Rick Down—to whom he would have to say a final good-bye, but tonight was not the night. He would see them over the winter, he was fairly sure of that. The hardest good-bye of all, he knew, would be the one he'd have to make to Joe, and he still wasn't sure how he was going to handle that. Even though he'd made his intentions known the week before, Joe had seemed to treat it as just another of those characteristic, shoot-from-the-hip outbursts from his emotional sidekick. Like all the others, it might continue to fester, but it wasn't to be taken at face value.

Had he ever been closer to any one person in all his years in baseball than Joe Torre?

Now he thought back to that first spring, in 1996, when they sat together on the bench and watched Derek Jeter taking grounders at short. There'd been reports—who knew where these things came from, other than someone looking to cover his ass with the boss?— that Jeter lacked the proper footwork to play shortstop in the majors. He and Joe just smiled. They'd needed barely a week to determine this kid, self-assured beyond his years, was ready to be the everyday shortstop for the New York Yankees. And when, on opening day in Cleveland, Jeter homered in his first at bat and made the game-saving over-the-head catch of Omar Vizquel's blooper in shallow center field, their initial, gut appraisal was validated. For the next eight years, Zim would serve as Jeter's willing foil—his head and belly to be rubbed for luck before each Jeter at bat; his shins to be peppered with deliberate short-hop tosses during pregame infield practice.

Jeter, as much as any of them, he'd come to think of as one of his own.

And it was the same with Mariano Rivera, the "ice man" reliever he'd also watched mature from a seemingly starstruck kid to a full-blown star overnight. In reflecting about Rivera, the funny thing was, he could barely remember the successes—they were all so methodical and automatic. It was those rare failures when the skinny Panamanian somehow lost a game that he had felt compelled to confront him. "Look," he'd tell him, "I don't ever want to see you getting down on yourself, pal. You must never forget it's because of you we're here. It's because of you we're what we are!"

Most of all, he remembered that night before the seventh game of the 2001 World Series against Arizona when, after Rivera finished his own brief, spiritual address to the team, Torre had then turned the floor over to the team trainer Gene Monahan. He loved Monahan, too, and that was the only time he could ever remember the trainer being asked to speak in a public team forum like this. He couldn't believe the inspiring words he heard out of Monahan that night. It was, he said, without elaborating, "one of the most moving speeches I'd ever heard in baseball."

"To have gotten to this point," Monahan began, "it's taken a fantastic effort and all of you guys have carried yourselves with the dignity and class that makes you Yankees. Believe me, you'll all be rewarded and heads will be held high in three hours because, to me, you're all champions no matter what the outcome. All of you have supported each other all season and we're all family here. And we've all had the benefit of an unbelievable coaching staff and this great manager."

Through all Zimmer's physical pain over those eight years—the bum knee, the foul-ball line drive off Chuck Knoblauch's bat into the dugout that struck him in the face, the groin pull he suffered in the one-punch knockdown scrap with Pedro Martinez—Monahan and his assistant, Steve Donohue, had been there to care for him. He always felt flattered they could not distinguish between him, a seventy-something coach and lifetime .235 hitter, and the $10-million-per-year player. Even though he realized it was their job to take care of everyone in the organization who was sent to them, he always figured they deserved extra compensation for tending to a broken-down old shortstop like him.

He finished changing into his street clothes and gently laid his Yankee pinstripes on the bench beside him. In the distance, he could hear the sound of voices of the other coaches coming down the aisle between their room and Joe's office. He felt his eyes begin to well up and quickly stiffened in an effort to compose himself. He would not allow anyone to see the sadness within him at having finally arrived at this moment. Grabbing his duffel bag, he headed out through the foyer of the coaches' room, only to find the small group of reporters waiting for him in the aisleway.

"I'm sorry guys," he said. "I got nothin' to say. I know I said the other day I would have somethin' to say, but I talked it over with my wife this morning and she was crying. I never seen her cry like that."

Anyway, they already knew why he was leaving, he thought, but just so they got it all right, he wanted them to know he was just leaving the Yankees, not baseball. "I just don't know who would want an old man like me," he said. "I'm going home and wait and see what happens."

He felt his eyes moistening again and he knew he had to get out of there. The reporters cleared the way for him as he executed a left turn and headed out the emergency exit door.

"Good luck, Zim," one of them called to him, but he didn't hear.

He was gone and the only thing surprising about it to him now was how uneventful the departure had really been. He'd half expected them to send a security guard down from the front office to personally escort him out of the stadium. Why not, he thought, one more slap in the face for the road? Of course, that would have hardly been necessary—the only things he was taking with him were his memories and his dignity.

# CHAPTER
# 1

## Just Treat Me Like a Human Being

I never wanted to leave the New York Yankees. At least not *when* I left them or *the way* I left them—after the 2003 season in which we won our sixth American League pennant in eight years and beat a Boston Red Sox team—that, on paper anyway, I thought was superior in what I felt was about the greatest, most gut-wrenching seven-game series I've ever been associated with. There are a lot of reasons why that American League Championship Series was as emotionally draining as it was—and that's also why I decided I'd just had enough.

I certainly wanted to be with Joe Torre through the final year of his contract as Yankee manager. We'd been through so much together, in a late-in-my-life relationship that I will cherish forever, and I never could have envisioned myself leaving Joe as I did. Maybe that's because I never could have envisioned having another guy I considered a friend for twenty-five years turning on me for no reason, which is what George Steinbrenner did, causing me to quit the Yankees.

I probably should have seen this coming, having been around Steinbrenner all those years and observing firsthand the way he treated people. My first experience with this was in December of 1983. Steinbrenner was in the process of changing managers, a common trait of his in those days. Clyde King had finished up the season as his third manager of the 1982 season, but it was common knowledge Steinbrenner was going to hire Billy Martin, who'd just been fired in Oakland, to manage the Yankees for the third time. In the meantime, George had hired me to be Billy's third base coach, which was okay by me, because during the course of the '82 season, Billy had asked me to coach for him in Oakland for 1983.

In any case, as the December winter meetings in Honolulu were approaching, Steinbrenner had still not told Clyde King that Billy Martin was going to be the new Yankee manager. Meanwhile, Steinbrenner called me and invited me and my wife, Soot, to come with him to Hawaii. In a sense, it was a free vacation since, as a coach for a manager who had not even been named yet, I didn't think I would have much work to do with whatever business the Yankees had there.

Well, George and I and our wives got on the plane in Tampa. It was one of those big 747s and right away there was some problem with the seats. George is raising hell with the woman ticket agent at the gate. We finally get on the plane and in the confusion, the wives wound up sitting together in one row of the first-class section with George and I behind them. I don't remember exactly what happened, other than the fact that George got involved in some conversation away from his seat and by the time he got back, the stewardess with the food cart had already left his dinner for him. It was prime rib—I do remember that—and by the time George got back, it was cold. Well, once again he starts ranting about his meal and I'm saying to myself, "What have I got myself into here?"

The next thing I know, he's sitting there next to me writing a letter to the president of American Airlines, detailing all these problems he's had with this flight to Hawaii.

But because he'd always been good to me—even our arguments were always good-natured—I suppose I blinded myself to the inevitability that this great run of Yankee championships we'd had since Joe took over as manager in 1996 would end badly. At least for some of us.

With Steinbrenner, there can never be happy endings because the man simply won't allow himself to be happy. Four world championships, six American League pennants, and eight straight trips to the postseason in eight years simply weren't good enough for him. The reason, I suppose, is because when we were winning those three straight world championships from 1998 to 2000—something I will assert right here will never be done again in this modern-day three-tiered postseason setup—Steinbrenner wasn't getting enough of the credit. Or at least he *thought* he wasn't getting enough of the credit, and, in his mind, Joe was getting *too much* of the credit. In any event, after we lost the 2001 World Series in Arizona, Steinbrenner finally had his opening. We had actually lost—with Mariano Rivera on the mound with a lead in the ninth inning, no less—and now Steinbrenner could start looking for people to blame.

I was told that immediately after the final out was recorded and the Diamondbacks were celebrating on their field, Steinbrenner was storming around the visiting clubhouse, making all sorts of threats about "big changes coming" as our players came in off the field. He also reportedly screamed at Phyllis Merhige, the woman from the American League office in charge of media relations, about television cameras being in the clubhouse before the game was over. I didn't see any of this—Joe, Derek Jeter, and I lingered awhile in the dugout and watched the Diamondbacks celebrate—but I'm told it was really awful. Anyway, looking back now, I think that was probably the beginning of the deterioration of relations between Steinbrenner and Joe's staff. It didn't matter that we'd had two of the most unbelievable sudden-death, extra-inning, comeback victories in baseball history in Games Four and Five at Yankee Stadium, or that this had been one of the most thrilling and memorable World Series ever. We didn't win and that was simply unacceptable.

As promised, Steinbrenner and his front office made a lot of changes for 2002, and while it was not entirely by design, there was no question in my mind the character and core of those championship Yankee teams began to change dramatically. Paul O'Neill and Scott Brosius retired and Tino Martinez, another strong character guy, was allowed to leave as a free agent without even so much as a "thanks for the memories" phone call from anyone because the decision had been made to sign Oakland's Jason Giambi, the defending American League MVP, to play first base.

We were able to win the AL East for the fifth straight season in 2002—by 10½ games—but in the first round of the playoffs, the best-of-five division series, we ran smack into a hot-hitting Anaheim Angels team that was putting it all together at just the right time. See, this is what Steinbrenner has never been able to understand. He thinks that spending more money on players should assure him of winning. It never occurs to him that maybe the guys on the other side of the field want to win, too. And when you get into these sudden-death, short postseason series, it doesn't matter a hoot what your players are earning.

I can't begin to recite all the things that went right for us in winning those four world championships—things that just as easily could have gone wrong. In baseball, the postseason is a crapshoot, especially that best-of-five first round. Anything can happen and may the hot team win—as was the case with the Angels in 2002.

So after winning the first game at Yankee Stadium, the Angels swept the next three, pounding our pitchers for a combined 44 hits and 26 runs. Steinbrenner didn't bother traveling with the team to Anaheim, but from his compound back in Tampa we knew he was seething and looking to lay the blame for this on Joe and the coaches. In the meantime, people had been asking me since the end of the regular season if I was coming back and my answer was always: "I'd like to, but you've gotta be asked." When the same people would then say: "Well, Joe wants you back," I'd say: "Maybe so, but he still has to answer to the people above him."

I had been told—and in the case of Billy Martin in 1983 when I was the Yankees' third base coach I'd seen it firsthand—that when Steinbrenner wants to get at his manager he starts off by going at it through his coaches. I figured there was a pretty good chance he'd take this loss to the Angels out on Joe's coaches. As it was, the season ended for us there in Anaheim, and we all went home not knowing if we had jobs for the following year. With most organizations I've been with, the coaches are always told whether they're coming back or not the last week of the season, or even sooner. At the very least, they're told to feel free to pursue other opportunities. We were told nothing in 2002, even though Joe was under contract for two more years.

Finally, about a week after the World Series, I got a call from Brian Cashman, the Yankee general manager, who pretty much confirmed my thinking of what Steinbrenner thought of us all.

"If you want to come back, you can," Cashman said. "But there are no raises for the coaches this year."

How's that for a backhanded way of being rehired! Not "We want you back" but rather "You can come back if you want." I sure did feel welcome to still be part of the New York Yankees. I told Cashman, "I'm not looking for no raise," and thanked him for the opportunity to remain on Joe's staff. Believe me, that's how it happened. I'm not smart enough to make this stuff up.

Of course, I'm sure Cashman was only putting it that way on orders from above. I can only imagine the abuse he had to take from Steinbrenner—and why a coach's bruised feelings might not exactly have been a high priority for him in his job as the boss's primary whipping boy. I came to realize that even more when I arrived at spring training and an embarrassed Cashman had to tell me my company car was being taken away from me. I'll get back to that in a minute.

Over the winter before the 2003 season, I spent much of my time, as always, at the Tampa Bay Downs racetrack, where I would periodically run into Steinbrenner. In the past, going back long before I worked for him, I'd see Steinbrenner at the track and he'd call me over to his table or he'd come over to my table where I sat with John "the Mailman" Colarusso. George and John had hit it off real good when they first met some years ago—George even took him to Saratoga one time. This one day that winter, I was sitting with John, and George was sitting at this little desk where Patti the hostess sat. He looked over at our table and said: "Hey, John, how are you doing?" He didn't say anything to me or acknowledge my presence. It was clear he was making a point of ignoring me.

A couple of days later, I was playing golf with Billy Connors, the Yankees' minor league pitching coach who is one of Steinbrenner's closest advisers in Tampa, and Gene "Stick" Michael, the chief Yankee scout. There had been some organization meetings earlier in the week, which Joe had attended, but not the coaches. Steinbrenner stopped inviting the coaches to these meetings after the first few years of Joe's term as manager. As we were playing golf, Billy suddenly said to me: "Boy, you won't believe how badly I got worked over from the boss yesterday."

"What happened?" I said.

"I'm not quite sure," Billy replied, "except that he's blaming me for leaking stuff to you that got into the *New York Post*."

"I'm not following you," I said.

"Well," Billy said, "at our meetings the other day we were discussing signing Contreras and somehow it got back to George King at the *Post*."

Now I was really confused. I had no idea what Billy was talking about. The only Contreras I knew was Nardi Contreras, who was related in some way to Lou Piniella and had been a pitching coach for a bunch of teams in the majors. It turned out Billy was talking about Jose Contreras, the Cuban pitcher who had escaped from Havana and was now a free agent. The Yankees wound up signing him for $32 million, outbidding the Red Sox a month later, but this whole thing about Steinbrenner thinking I had told George King—who happens to be a friend—about the Yankees' interest in him was nuts.

"I told him that," Billy insisted, "but someone told him you talk to George King a lot and he looked at me and said: 'That figures. You told Zimmer and he told King.'"

The fact was, not only did I not know anything about Jose Contreras, I hadn't talked to King since the season ended. I can't remember ever talking to King in the off-season. But coming as this did, shortly after Cashman's cold phone call and Steinbrenner making a point to ignore me at the track, it was becoming pretty clear I had somehow gone from the very short list of Steinbrenner friends to a considerably lengthy one of people he considers enemies.

I could only laugh. This guy is simply unbelievable. He talks about loyalty and friendship like they're what he's all about.

About ten years ago, before I was a Yankee, Steinbrenner came to me one winter and asked me if I would come to this breakfast he was having at the Bay Harbor, his hotel in Tampa, for his Gold Shield Foundation, which raised money for the families of police and firefighters killed in the line of duty. I started going every year for him and one year I was even the chief speaker. There was always this big, round table with nothing but Yankee people at it along with George and his family. Then about three years ago, I showed up at the breakfast and the only ones at the Yankee table were Bill Emslie, another of Steinbrenner's chief advisers in the minor league complex, and his wife. I said to him: "Where are all the Yankees? I've been doing this every year for George."

I was later told that Steinbrenner got his nose out of joint because the Tampa police had arrested Darryl Strawberry, whom he was trying to save from a life of drugs. I don't know how true that was, but it was apparent George no longer had anything to do with this breakfast. I just wish somebody had bothered to tell me. I was showing up every year and giving my time out of my friendship with him. I have to admit to being baffled at the way Steinbrenner operates, as well as at his strange sense of loyalty.

I happen to like both Doc Gooden and Strawberry, who, despite their very public problems with drugs, were given new leases on life by Steinbrenner with six-figure jobs as instructors in the minor league complex in Tampa. His generosity and compassion toward them has been overwhelming and yet, I think even both of them would have to agree, they've done nothing but embarrass him with their repeated brushes with the law. On the other hand, the people working in New York—from Cashman to Joe and the coaches, the trainers, and all the front office people who have served the Yankees with honor and diligence—get no thanks and only angry abuse from him while working under the constant threat of being fired at his whim.

One of the highlights of every winter in Tampa is the annual Gasparilla Parade. In 2003 the parade organizers chose as the grand marshal Steinbrenner's son-in-law Steve Swindal, who is also one of the general partners of the Yankees. I got a call from Billy Connors asking me if I would do Steve a favor by going on the Yankee float. I guess Steve wasn't aware that I was no longer in favor with his father-in-law. Like a dummy, I said yes and I wound up on the float with Gooden and our bullpen coach Rich Monteleone (who lives in Tampa). That was it. For whatever reason, no one else from the organization was there. Our principal duty was to toss out these foam baseballs to the crowds lined up along Bayshore Boulevard. There was a stiff wind blowing that day and I'm throwing these balls into it. The next day I couldn't raise my arm and it hasn't been the same since. Chalk it up as another battle scar of my last year with the Yankees.

I arrived in spring training one day early because we had to get our physicals at a doctor's office rather than the ballpark where we'd always gotten them before. We had a noon meeting at Legends Field, but we were done with our physicals early and decided to go to our favorite breakfast place, Mom's, on Dale Mabry Highway about a half mile north of the ballpark. It was just Monteleone, Lee Mazzilli, Mel Stottlemyre, and me. As we were having breakfast, Monteleone happened to mention that his wife had to drive him to the park because the Yankees weren't giving him a car for spring training anymore.

"Don't worry," I said. "I've got a car waiting for me in the parking lot at the ballpark. If somehow you don't get a car, you can have mine."

We got to the park about eleven o'clock and Cashman greeted us.

"There's something I need to talk to you about," he said to me. "George came over this morning and looked through all the rental cars and he pulled your car."

I think Cash thought I was gonna get hot and maybe quit right there.

"You want to put that by me again?" I said.

"He's pulled your car," Cashman repeated.

"That's good," I said and walked away.

Later, I saw Monteleone in the coaches' room and said: "About that car, Monty. I don't have one."

Well, it didn't take long for my car situation to spread all over spring training. A couple, of days later, I got a call from my pal, Jimmy Leyland, the former Pittsburgh Pirates and Florida Marlins manager who was now coaching in spring training for the St. Louis Cardinals over in Jupiter, on the east coast.

"I just wanted you to know, Popeye, that we're taking up a collection over here to get you a new car so you can get around the camps over there," Leyland said. "Your friends are really coming through for you!"

Phillies coach John Vukovich, another of my oldest friends, also couldn't wait to chime in.

"So what are you doing now, sleeping in the ballpark?" he said. "They got taxis, you know."

When Joe heard about Steinbrenner pulling my car he just shook his head. I told him: "I'll bet you in two days someone will say I got my car back."

Sure enough, a few days later when I went to see the traveling secretary, David Szen, to pick up my meal money. I said: "Am I entitled to this or is he taking meal money away from me too?"

Szen laughed, then replied that there had been a change and that I would have a car after all. I told him: "Thanks, David, but I have my own car. Tell him he can take the keys to this one and stuff them up his behind."

I was now seeing firsthand just how petty and vindictive Steinbrenner can be once he decides he doesn't like someone. What I didn't know was that this was just the beginning.

Before spring training, Debbie Tymon, the Yankees vice president of marketing, called me from New York to ask my permission about having a Don Zimmer Bobblehead Doll Day at Yankee Stadium the coming season. I said: "Great! That sounds like terrific fun." Then, thinking about the old army helmet I had worn the day after getting whacked by a foul ball in the dugout a couple of years earlier, I said: "Anyway we could do it with the helmet?"

"We're already ahead of you," she said. "That's the plan."

I could tell by the tone of Debbie's voice she was really excited about this idea and so was I. Naturally, I immediately told my kids and all of my grandkids and started making arrangements to buy up a hundred or so of the dolls to give to them and my friends. That first week, after we'd gotten home to New York to start the season, I was sitting in the dugout when Debbie came up to me and said: "I hate to tell you this, Don, but we've had to cancel your bobblehead doll day."

"What happened?" I said.

"Oh," she said, "there was something about a problem with the company and we had to do another bobblehead day with Hideki Matsui."

I didn't quite get the drift of it and I just said: "That's fine. I'm sorry."

When I got home that night, I started thinking about all this and I said to myself: "I wonder if he got his nose into this too? And if so, why would he do something like that if it would help the club?" As it was, they had originally planned to have my bobblehead day on a day we were playing Detroit.

I waited for another week or ten days before approaching Debbie about it again.

"Debbie," I said, "I've got to ask you something. You know that bobblehead day for me they canceled? Did George have anything to do with it?"

Have you ever seen little kids who do something wrong in the house and you can just tell by their expression? Well, when I asked her this, she didn't know what to say and she answered me again with something like, "No, it was the company." However, the expression on her face told me she wasn't leveling with me. Still, I was just guessing. But I do know that from that day on, Debbie Tymon never looked at me again—and she and I had been pals. I was always in the dugout early before games when she'd be out there with her little promotion groups and she'd come over and sit with me and shoot the breeze for a half hour.

Then, after the season was over, Cashman called me to thank me for all I'd done for the Yankees and for the help I'd given Joe and so forth. I thought that was a real nice gesture and before we said our good-byes, I said: "Cash, I gotta ask you a question. They were supposed to have a bobblehead day with me. Can you tell me what happened?"

He said: "Yeah, we had it programmed on one of the days we were going to play Detroit. We figured we were gonna have twenty thousand, but with Don Zimmer bobbleheads we could make it forty thousand. But George wouldn't go for it. I tried to tell George how much money we could get for it, but he wouldn't buy it."

So then I knew that I was right about Debbie Tymon not being straight with me, which I feel bad about. I feel bad about it for her; that she can't be forthright—to people who were her friends because of him.

Nevertheless, I guess I never imagined how truly wacky this guy was until an incident that occurred in early May. By now, between the winter snubs, the rescinded car in spring training, and the canceled bobblehead doll night, there was no doubt Steinbrenner would do anything to force me to quit. It was at the end of our second homestand I got sick, stricken with what they later said was diverticulitis. I was sick for four days and had to go to Beth Israel Hospital in Manhattan. In the meantime, the Yankees were going to the West Coast for a six-game series against Seattle and Oakland. I wanted to go, but the doctors insisted I had to stay in New York and get my rest; that the trip to the West Coast would take too much out of me.

Get my rest? How was I supposed to do that when I was sitting at home watching all of our games on TV until two in the morning?

It didn't help either that we were in the throes of a mini–losing streak, having lost our last two games at home and the first game in Seattle against the Mariners. In that game, Andy Pettitte got knocked around for 8 runs and 9 hits in just 4⅓ innings (although only 4 of the runs were earned as our defense committed 3 errors in the game). But it turned out to be one of those brutal games where everything Joe did, especially with the pitching, just didn't work out.

The next morning, I'm sitting in my apartment in Westchester and my cell phone rings. Only a very few people know my cell phone number so naturally I answered it right away. On the other end, I hear this unmistakable voice—Steinbrenner.

"What are you doing?" he says.

"I'm all right," I said.

"Well," he says, "I'll tell you one thing. You better get your ass on a plane to Oakland for the weekend because my manager and my pitching coach don't know what the hell they're doing."

I was both stunned and hurt. Stunned because I couldn't believe this guy was calling me after all he'd done to embarrass and humiliate me since last winter, and hurt because of the statement he made about my manager and our pitching coach. I didn't say anything to him, but after hanging up the phone, I did what I was told by him and called David Szen in Seattle and asked him to book me on a plane to Oakland the next day. For all I knew, Steinbrenner was hoping I'd get sick again and *that* would force me to quit.

Awhile later, Cashman called me and said: "What the hell is going on here?"

"I'm going to Oakland tomorrow morning," I said, not telling him about the phone call from Steinbrenner.

Then Dr. Stuart Hershon, the Yankee team physician, called me and said: "Don, I've talked to the other two doctors who administered to you and they said you can't go on this trip." Cashman followed that up with another call to me, telling me I couldn't go on the trip and that was what happened.

The papers reported that I'd tried to come back to the team but was overruled by the doctors. No one, not even Joe, ever knew the real reason I made arrangements to fly to the West Coast. How goofy is this man Steinbrenner? He's sitting home there in Tampa, frustrated and upset over us losing a couple of games on the West Coast, and he's so mad at Joe and Mel, he calls me—the SOB he wants to get rid of—and tells me to get out there because they can't do the job. It's almost scary. But it leaves me no doubt about what, and who, was behind those vicious attacks Steinbrenner's pal, Al Neuharth, took at Joe in *USA Today* during the 2003 season. Neuharth, I'm told, was the founder of *USA Today,* which I guess makes him one of the big shots who get to sit in Steinbrenner's private box. All I know is the things he wrote about Joe sounded exactly like the things I'd heard Steinbrenner say about Joe. Where else would Neuharth come up with those kinds of mean-spirited and downright dumb opinions? He had to hear them somewhere.

Steinbrenner had begun taking veiled shots at Joe and the coaches the previous winter when, in an article in the *Daily News,* he criticized Derek Jeter for too much late-night partying and said that the coaches were going to have work harder in 2003. As the season progressed, it seemed every time we lost a couple of games, Steinbrenner would be quoted in the papers saying things like "this is Joe's team" and "we gave him everything he wanted." All the while, the speculation continued that he was getting ready to fire Joe. It was insane.

Joe, for his part, didn't respond to all of this, except in April when Steinbrenner pushed him too far by overruling his decision to send Contreras to Columbus. Because all five of our starters were pitching well, we had no choice but to begin using Contreras out of the bullpen—with mixed results. Finally there was a meeting of the minds as to what to do with him so he could get more regular work. Steinbrenner initially had told Joe the decision was Joe's and Joe thought it was best to send Contreras to Columbus. But after Joe told Contreras that was what we were going to do, Steinbrenner announced that we were instead sending him to Tampa so he can work with Billy Connors. This was not only embarrassing to Joe but it was a direct slap at Mel Stottlemyre, who'd been working with Contreras and had already prepared a work program for him at Columbus.

Then in late May, this story comes out with George blasting the coaches again and one picture in the paper has these six ducks with our faces on them—as in lame ducks. So we all got copies of the paper and signed our names on them. That was the day I went to an autograph signing at a shoe store downtown and Michael Kay was doing his radio show out of there, which I didn't know. While I'm there, Kay asks me to come on his show to talk about this story.

"What about all this hullabaloo yesterday?" he asked me and I said: "Well, he's done nothing but blast all the coaches since the middle of the winter. For seven years when we were winning, it was his and Tampa's team but now 'cause we're losing, it's Joe's team."

I went on to say that I thought that was unfair. That was my statement—unfair. Then I got to the ballpark and—boom!—everybody's there wanting to ask me questions. I more or less told them what I told Michael Kay—that when we win, it's George and Tampa and when we lose, it's Joe Torre's team. That's when somebody said to me: "Do you think you'll get in trouble for saying all this?"

I said: "I don't know. The boss is the boss. He can say what he wants, which he does. But what does that mean I'm supposed to do? Crawl into a hole like a mouse?"

Well, the next day they had this big cartoon of a mouse on the front page of the *Post* with my face on it and the headline: THE MOUSE THAT ROARED.

Naturally, the writers all went to Steinbrenner to get his reaction and he tried to downplay everything, saying he didn't know what I said and wouldn't react to it. Anyone who knows the man, knows that was a crock and a couple of days later, I found out just how much of a crock it was.

We'd gone back on the road for three games in Detroit and now we were in Cincinnati getting ready for a three-game series against the Reds. I'm sitting in my hotel room when I get a call from my pal, Tom Villante, who used to head up baseball's national TV operation when Bowie Kuhn was the commissioner.

"Are you okay?" Villante said.

"Yeah, I'm all right," I answered, "why?"

"Well, did you and Joe have a riff?" he continued.

"What are you talking about?" I asked.

"I don't see you next to him on TV anymore," Villante said.

"I don't know what you're talking about," I said. "I'm next to him every minute of the game."

"Well, I haven't seen you in three days," he said.

This is when the story came out that Steinbrenner had sent orders to his TV company—the YES Network—to supposedly put Joe in a 'box' when they panned the camera on the dugout so you couldn't see anybody sitting next to him. The next thing I hear is that the announcers were told not to use my name on the YES station. During all this, as I said, we're in Cincinnati, which is my hometown, and from there we're going to Wrigley Field in Chicago where I managed. That first day in Cincinnati, somebody told me that when Paul O'Neill sat down by his microphone, there was a note that said: "Don't use Zimmer on the station." Paul doesn't know what's going on. He was kind of a fill-in announcer and didn't travel with us very much.

Later, I'm on the field and I hear that Jim Kaat, the main YES announcer, had called someone at the YES Network and said: "I can't do my job with this order. This guy lived in Cincinnati and was Manager of the Year in Chicago. How can I not talk about him?"

Supposedly, the guy told Kaat: "Well, just don't use his name. You'll get me fired."

I think Kaat then went to somebody even higher and told him that if he couldn't use my name he might as well take a leave of absence. After that, it seemed, somebody lifted the ban. Even the players came up to me and joked about the ban being lifted.

But while the ban may have been lifted, Steinbrenner's agenda with the coaches hardly was.

One day around the middle of the season, we were all sitting in the coaches' room early in the afternoon, before most of the players had arrived, when a kid came down from the front office with some sort of message for Joe. I'm not exactly sure what it was he was sent down there for, but before he left he told us he'd been ordered by Steinbrenner that, above all, he was not to go into the coaches' room. "I don't want you talking to those assholes," is how we were told Steinbrenner put it to him.

Well, after all he'd said and done to us, that was pretty much the clincher as far as I was concerned. From that day on, we all began sarcastically referring to each other as "asshole" and, if nothing else, I think it kind of bonded us even more. All the while, though, I kept asking myself: "What kind of a screwed-up operation is this that, after eight straight trips to the postseason and four world championships, we've got an owner here who thinks the coaches are nothing but a bunch of assholes?" Sad.

There's a reason I'd spent fifty-four years in baseball. I love the game and I always had fun. In 2003, George Steinbrenner took the fun out of it for me, in the same way he took the fun out of it for so many other good baseball people like Yogi Berra, Dick Howser, and Bob Lemon, to name three. It's really a shame. We were good friends—I was the one guy who could kid with him. Other people were mostly scared of him, but not me. He'd come into Joe's office with that stern look on his face and I'd say: "Hey, boss, how's your personality today?" To this day, I still don't know what it was I did to him to have him turn on me and treat me like he did.

Late in the 2003 season, they had a day for Ron Guidry, and sometime earlier in the year they'd interviewed me to say a few words about him. I love Guidry. He's a real pal, and that's why I made sure I got out there early that day and on the top step of the dugout where I could see all the proceedings. Throughout the presentations, they kept showing different people up on the big scoreboard, talking about Guidry. And for about a minute or so, they had me up there. After the game, I'm in the parking lot about to get into my car when one of the kids who works at the stadium comes up to me and says, "Mr. Zimmer, I have to tell you something. You won't believe what happened up there today."

It turned out that right after they showed my little tribute statement to Guidry, the kids were called on the carpet by Lonn Trost, one the team vice presidents. According to the kid, Trost was screaming about me being on the scoreboard, saying: "You know how much George hates Zimmer!"

It's almost funny if it wasn't so sick. But this is why I left the Yankees. It was after we beat the Red Sox in the ALCS that I had a sort of personal "bloodletting" in which I unleashed all my anger at what had been going on all year. I had planned to wait until after the World Series, but there was so much emotion attached to that Red Sox series, and when a reporter approached me in the coaches' room and asked me how I felt after we'd finally won, it was like everything inside of me erupted. I never intended to be a distraction for the World Series, which is why I made it known to the media I wasn't going to talk about anything except baseball until everything was officially over.

Even though we'd all left just about everything out there on the field in the Red Sox series (myself obviously included), I believed, as Joe did, that we had enough left to beat the Marlins in the Series. In retrospect, we were wrong. The Series turned out to be a matchup of a hot team that was playing with the house's money against a veteran team that had been there plenty of times before. Those other times, however, we'd almost always gotten the big hit or the big break when we needed it. Against the Marlins in 2003, that didn't happen.

I sensed the Series starting to turn after Game Four in which Roger Clemens got roughed up for 5 hits and 3 runs all with 2 out in the first inning, before settling down and pitching shutout ball over the next six. We came back to tie that game like the Yankees of old on Ruben Sierra's 2-out pinch-hit triple in the ninth inning. But we failed to cash in on a bases-loaded, 1-out situation in the eleventh, and then Jeff Weaver gave up the game-winning homer to Marlin shortstop Alex Gonzalez leading off the twelfth.

I know there was a lot of criticism of Joe for using Weaver—who'd had a rocky year for us—in that situation, but who else was he supposed to use? The whole reason Weaver was on the postseason roster was because we might need a pitcher to give us innings and Joe had already used Jose Contreras and Jeff Nelson. He brought Weaver in to start the eleventh against the heart of the Marlin order—Jeff Conine, Mike Lowell, and Derrek Lee, the first two being right-handed hitters. Weaver got them out 1-2-3, and once he did that, he was certainly coming back for the twelfth. Who knew how long the game was going to go? As far as I'm concerned, that game was lost when we didn't score in the eleventh.

And then the Series really turned in Game Five when "Boomer" Wells's back gave out after just one inning. It wasn't until a few minutes before the game that anyone knew Wells was hurting. Joe came to me and said: "Wells might not be able to make it tonight." I thought: What can you do? You go with what you got. When Wells came in after retiring the Marlins in the first and said he'd had it, Joe had no choice but to bring in Contreras and hope for the best, that he could give us enough innings to get us to the short men in the bullpen. I've got to say Contreras, whom Steinbrenner had signed for $32 million the previous winter, was a bit of a puzzlement to us. At times, like in Game Four, he'd show a great slider and breaking pitch and look like the pitcher they'd said was the number-one guy in Cuba before he defected. Then, on other times, he'd battle with his command and seemed to lose confidence in his pitches. That was unfortunately the case in Game Five.

Contreras started out okay, getting the first two Marlin batters in the second inning, but then he walked the next two guys and gave up a double to Gonzalez on an 0-1 pitch to tie the score 1–1. Now there were runners at second and third and the pitcher, Brad Penny, coming up. I don't ever like to second-guess—as this is going to sound—but there are times when you've just got to use common sense. I was sitting there watching this all unfold and I said to myself: "I hope to hell this guy doesn't throw a fastball here." If there's one pitch a pitcher can hit, it's a fastball and, sure enough, if that isn't what Contreras threw Penny, who hit a humpback liner into right-center field for 2 runs and a 3–1 Marlin lead we never over-came. To me, that pitch was the turning point of the whole Series. We rallied late, but once again not enough, and lost 6–4. Two nights later, back at Yankee Stadium, Josh Beckett defied all the critics of Marlin manager Jack McKeon for pitching him on three days rest and shut us out on 5 hits to end the Series.

By this time, I'd had second thoughts about making any "farewell address" after the Series was over. I'd said my piece earlier and everyone pretty much knew why I was leaving. I loved the players. I loved the manager. And I will always love New York and all the fans there. I was out of there only because of one person. A few days later, after my quitting had become official, Yogi called me and tried to get me to reconsider.

"Ah," he said, "just forget it. You'll both get over it."

"Forget it? Get over it?" I laughed. "*You're* a fine one to talk! It took you fourteen years to get over what he did to you!"

# CHAPTER

## 2

# Beanballs
# and
# Haymakers

Y ou might wonder what would possess a seventy-two-year-old coach to run out onto a baseball field in the middle of melee and throw a haymaker at a player some forty years his junior? I've been asked this question maybe about a hundred times since that October Saturday afternoon at Fenway Park when I made a bull's rush at Pedro Martinez in the middle of Game Three of the 2003 Yankees-Red Sox American League Championship Series—and got myself slam-dunked onto the grass in something that looked like a scene right out of the World Wrestling Federation.

To say the least, it was not one of the prouder moments of my fifty-four years in baseball. Every time I see that clip of me being hurled to the ground by Pedro I feel embarrassed, as well I should be. It was just plain stupid of me and I was lucky I didn't get hurt a lot worse than I did, walking away with a pulled groin and a bunch of aching muscles. But I have always been a man of impulse, at least when it comes to being pushed to the limit by people who I believe have done me or my friends wrong. I did, after all, quit baseball in the middle of the fifth inning of a game when I was bench coach for the Colorado Rockies in 1995, and Joe Torre has never let me forget the time in the Metrodome in Minnesota in 1996 when I went into a rage with umpire Greg Bonin, who'd accused me of being on drugs! Nobody had ever said anything like that to me and, as I told the writers afterward, if I'd had it to do all over again, I'd have punched Bonin in the nose.

That was the way I felt about Pedro Martinez.

Though certainly not by my choice, my baseball life has sort of been defined by beanballs—I was twice nearly killed by pitches to my head—so when these sorts of incidents occur, I have my opinions about them. In all cases, however, I have never pretended to know a pitcher's true intentions. Only the pitcher himself knows whether he's deliberately trying to hurt somebody or merely establishing his "turf" when it comes to maintaining an advantage over the hitters.

My confrontation with Pedro Martinez was really the culmination of a series of incidents involving him that had been going on with the Yankees and Red Sox for over a year. I've watched Pedro pitch.

He's one of the two or three best in all of baseball. He's got pinpoint control and can throw a pitch into a tea cup. I've seen him throw at people's heads and I've seen him knock guys down. He knocked out our second baseman, Alfonso Soriano, and our shortstop, Derek Jeter, in the same inning of a game in Boston with pitches in on their hands. Was he trying to hurt them? I can't say, although in both cases, they're guys who lean over the plate and Pedro's a pitcher who isn't going to allow hitters to do that. Soriano stands close to the plate and Jeter's a diver who goes into the ball a lot. It's not tough to hit either one of them on the arm.

I stood right on top the plate, too, like Soriano, and I got hit on the arms and wrists a bunch of times. One in particular I still remember was when I was with the Washington Senators and Ike Delock, another Red Sox pitcher, hit me right on my funny bone. You always want to be a tough guy and not give the pitcher the satisfaction of letting him know how much it hurts. Don Baylor, who holds the lifetime record of most times hit by a pitch, 262, was the absolute best at this. Baylor could be hit right smack in the flesh of his arm, wrist, or back and never even flinch. So I walked to first base and stood there, refusing to rub it. But I can say now, I felt like I was going to throw up. It hurt that bad. That's why you never heard me say anything about Pedro hitting our two guys like that, even though there was quite an uproar when Jeter and Soriano had to miss a few games.

My beef with Pedro went back to the 2002 season in a game he wasn't even pitching, at Yankee Stadium. It was one of those typical Yankee–Red Sox games with a lot of tension in the air and, throughout, Pedro was standing on the top step of their dugout yelling stuff over at us, especially when Jorge Posada was batting. I don't know what he was saying, but he was pointing to his ears and his behind as if to say Posada had big ears or a big behind or something. It was clear he was taunting him and I just thought that was one of the most unprofessional things I'd ever seen on a ball field. To be honest, I was frankly a little surprised the Red Sox manager, Grady Little, didn't put a stop to it.

It wasn't just that game, either. It seemed every time we played the Red Sox and Pedro wasn't pitching, he'd be up there on the top step of the dugout chirping at Posada.

So now we come to that third game of the ALCS when Pedro is pitching and everything is going along fine for the first few innings, living up to all the expectations of the hyped Pedro-Roger Clemens matchup. But in the fourth, Pedro began to unravel a little as we went ahead 4–2 on a 2-run double by Hideki Matsui. Suddenly, Pedro was in danger of an early KO, with runners at second and third and nobody out. This was hardly the time to lose your cool but, sure enough, Pedro did. He hit Karim Garcia in the back with a pitch—I can only guess out of anger and frustration over giving up the lead the Red Sox had provided him.

Later, Joe told the media there was no question in his mind that Pedro hit Garcia on purpose, and I'd have to say there was little question in anyone else's mind either that it was deliberate. Garcia, for his part, did the right thing by sliding hard into second base on a ground ball double play, knocking over Red Sox second baseman Todd Walker. This was nothing more than good hard-nosed baseball, and it's about the only way hitters in the American League—with the DH rule that protects pitchers from having to come to bat—can get a return pound of flesh after being deliberately hit. As Garcia came into our dugout, guys patted him in on the back, including Posada.

Meanwhile, Pedro was standing on the mound jawing at Posada again, only now he was pointing to his head as if to say: "You're next and it's coming right at your head."

I'm watching all of this and now I'm starting to really get hot. By this time, I'd already gotten pretty tired of Pedro's act, as had our players. Nerves were getting more and more frayed, which was never more evident than when Manny Ramirez led off the bottom of the fourth for Boston, and Clemens threw a pitch high and just a shade inside that made him livid. To see Manny's reaction, you'd have thought Clemens had drilled him between the eyes when, in fact, the pitch was almost a strike. David Ortiz, who was in the on-deck circle, immediately tried to calm Manny down, but it was too late. The benches and the bullpens started clearing out and all of sudden we had ourselves a good old-fashioned baseball brawl going on.

I came up onto the field, looked around and said to myself: "Where's Pedro?" Then I saw him coming up out of their dugout. I thought: "This is my one shot to take a swipe at him."

Obviously, this wasn't a very rational thought, but like I said, I was hot and this had been building up inside of me for nearly a year. I couldn't get the picture of Pedro taunting Posada out of my mind. That and the fact that Pedro had stood there and pointed at Posada, telling the world he was going to throw at him. I don't know how the umpire had let him stay in the game after that.

So I make my run at Pedro, but as I go to throw my punch, the next thing I know I'm rolling around on the ground. It all happened so fast, I didn't have time to realize what a fool I'd made of myself and how my family, sitting in the seats watching this, must have felt, seeing me thrown to the ground like that. My wife, Soot, told me later that she didn't see what happened, but my granddaughter,

Whitney, sitting with her, saw the whole thing and was really upset. Whitney screamed: "Grammy! Pedro just threw Poppy to the ground! He's hurt!"

A few rows away, some Red Sox fan sitting behind my daughter, Donna, got up and started screaming: "Kill him! Kill Zimmer!"

Donna, who has never forgotten being in Fenway Park as a kid in the late 1970s when I was the Red Sox manager and getting booed regularly, turned around to him and said: "Nice, real nice. That's my dad."

As I was lying there on the ground, a guy came up to me, leaned over, and said: "Are you okay?" It was Todd Jones, one of the Red Sox relief pitchers. I thought that was a really nice gesture.

The next inning after the brawl, I'm standing on the top step of the dugout next to Joe Torre, and Ortiz is on third base for the Red Sox. I remember there was a time-out for some reason and I notice that Ortiz is looking into our dugout. I just happened to be looking at him and all of a sudden he nods his head. Now we've got a lot of guys sitting there and I turned around to see if there's somebody behind me that he's nodding at, only there's no one. I looked back at him and he pointed at me and gave me a thumbs-up sign. I took that to mean, "Are you okay?" That, I thought, was also pretty nice. Remember, this guy was probably Pedro's closest friend on the team.

After the game, Dr. Hershon told me I had to go to the hospital. I didn't want to go, but apparently for insurance purposes they had to take a bunch of X rays to make sure I hadn't broken my hip. They put me on a stretcher to take my blood pressure and that was the way they wanted to take me out of the ballpark to the ambulance— like I was half dead. I couldn't talk them out of it, so there I was being carted out of Fenway Park on a stretcher. In the meantime, my family was all waiting for me at the Capital Grille downtown for dinner. It turned out they put me through a whole bunch of tests and X rays and now it was nearly ten o'clock by the time I got released from the hospital. A cop I knew from my managing days in Boston was there at the hospital with us and he gave me and Soot a ride down to the restaurant.

As I walked in, the place was still packed with people, just about all of them Red Sox fans. Naturally, I was a little worried, but as I worked my way through the restaurant to the back where my family was just starting dessert, people started clapping. Then this guy grabs me. It's Todd Jones. I stopped and thanked him for his concern back out there on the field. The next step I took, another guy grabs me. It's Tim Wakefield, the Red Sox knuckleball pitcher who held us to 2 runs in Game One and would then come back to beat us again in Game Four. He shakes my hand and now my head is really spinning. I can't believe these guys. That's what makes baseball so special to me. The people in it—and not just your teammates.

I finally got to my table and the waiter comes over and says. "The guy over there wants to buy a bottle of wine for you."

I looked over to where he was pointing and it was Wakefield, who was smiling and waving to me again.

"Tell him, no thanks, I'd rather have the cash!" I said to the waiter.

A few minutes later, Wakefield walks over to my table and hands me his wallet!

The next day, Pedro sent word to me that he wanted to apologize. I said: "What does he have to apologize for? I was the guy who charged him and threw the punch." To the people who said Pedro beat up an old man I said, no, an old man was dumb enough to try and beat up on Pedro.

It was me who had to do the apologizing—which I did in a very abbreviated press conference before the Sunday game was rained out. I didn't apologize to Pedro, however. I apologized to the media for not talking to them and explaining myself after we'd won the game the day before, and I apologized to the Yankees, the Red Sox, the fans, the umpires, and most of all to my family for being such an embarrassment to them. Like I said, it was not my finest moment and I wish it never happened. My punishment will be having to watch that film clip and looking at that picture of me rolling around on the infield grass of Fenway Park for the rest of my life.

That said, I think now would be a good time to talk a little more about beanballs, headhunters, and pitchers just being aggressive and what I consider to be the difference.

Whenever people talk about supposed head-hunting pitchers, the first name that almost always comes up is Don Drysdale, my teammate with the Dodgers from 1956 to 1959. When "Big D" first came up to the Dodgers in 1956 he was no wider than one of those palm trees out there in the outfield of Holman Stadium in Vero Beach. We had a very powerful lineup and we were also better than other teams because we had guys like Gil Hodges, Duke Snider, and Roy Campanella hitting home runs. At the same time, because they were hitting so many homers, there were pitchers always taking free shots at them. I'm talking about beanballs. The game is not the same today as it was then. There was more of it back then, probably because of the designated hitter, but a lot too because of the camaraderie of today's players. Drysdale would see Campy get turned inside out or Hodges get knocked on his rear end, and if he was pitching in that game, he would never say anything about knocking anybody down. Later on, his theory was: "I'm gonna get two for every one! If they want to knock down one of our hitters, then I'm gonna knock two of theirs down." And he was respected real early in his career by his teammates.

Drysdale, God rest his soul, was known as a headhunter, but people don't realize where it started. He did it to protect his own players and he did a pretty good job of it. And if Pee Wee Reese were alive today, or Campy or Hodges, they'd tell you the same thing. They respected him and they loved him.

Tom Seaver tells a story about how he had to protect his hitters against Bob Gibson, who was as notorious as Drysdale for knocking guys down. In August of 1972, Seaver was pitching for the Mets against the Cardinals in a game in St. Louis. The score was tied 2–2 when Seaver came to bat in the ninth inning with a runner on first base.

"It was an obvious bunt situation," Seaver recalled, "and Gibby of course dropped me on the first pitch with a ball right under my helmet."

The following spring, Gibson was pitching against the Mets in St. Petersburg when John Milner hit doubles in the first and third innings off him. In the fifth inning when Milner came up, Gibson took two shots at him, the second one hitting him squarely in the left shoulder.

"Right then and there I knew I was going to have to retaliate," Seaver said. "I wasn't pitching that day so I didn't know when or where. I just knew Gibby was going to get his."

On April 12 that year Gibson and Seaver hooked up again and, with the Mets leading 2–0, Gibson came to bat for the first time. According to Seaver, after getting two quick strikes, he threw one close pitch to Gibson that everyone ignored. The next one, however, was right at Gibson's chin, spinning him around until he landed in an awkward position on the ground in front of the plate.

"You're control is better than that, Tommy," Gibson yelled at Seaver.

"I know it is," Seaver said he replied. "I was just remembering the ball you threw under my helmet last year!"

I know how it was with me. I used to stand right in there on top of the plate and I'd swing real hard and miss and damn near fall down doing it and the pitcher would come halfway off the mound and yell: "You little pisspot. You ain't gonna swing like that off of me." That was the only swing I knew, but the next pitch would be at my head. That's just the way it was in those days. You didn't get offended like the way players today get when a pitch is even just a little too close. At the same time, one of the things I have never been able to understand in all my years in baseball is how a guy hits a home run and the next guy gets knocked down. I've watched this going on for years and years and I've never been able to understand what goes through a pitcher's mind to knock the next guy down instead of the guy who hit the home run!

I'll give you an example of how pitchers used to think when I was playing. I was with the Dodgers in a game against the Reds in Crosley Field in Cincinnati. It was 1956. The Reds pitcher was Rudy Minarcin and I hit a ball off him that bounces off the center field fence. I make it into third with a head-first slide for a triple. Minarcin strikes the next batter out to end the inning and then I had to walk by him to get my glove. He came right at me and yelled: "You won't be hitting any more off the center field fence. You'll be hitting off the back of your ass. I guarantee it!" Now I was hitting .230 or something at the time and I said to him: "Ain't I ever supposed to get a hit?" But that was the mentality of pitchers back then. Can you imagine pitchers telling you they're gonna knock you down because you swung too hard? Like I said, I didn't know how to swing any other way!

Drysdale used to say, "The easiest pitch to get out of the way of is the one coming right at your head." I can't say I disagree with that. If you're standing there at the plate and the pitcher throws one right at your ribs, you can't decide which way to go.

I can't say if pitchers like Drysdale crossed the line by deliberately throwing at guys' heads. I would guess that maybe he did a few times, I think, because there were simply more knockdowns back then. Another one was Early Wynn, who unfortunately also isn't here anymore to defend himself. Early was a great pitcher. He was also a big man, like Drysdale, who could be very intimidating. Because he was a big man, he didn't move real well and he didn't like people bunting on him. His way of letting you know he didn't like you bunting on him was to throw one right at you—a knockdown, if you will. I only faced Early at the end of his career, but I seem to remember getting knocked down by him in spring training. It didn't matter to him what the game situation was. He considered it a personal insult if you bunted on him.

I suppose when the humpties like myself got a rare lick off some of these pitchers, it was particularly annoying to them. The good hitters, however, all knew a good day at the plate might very well come at a price. One I particularly remember was Joe Adcock, the big right-handed-hitting first baseman for the Milwaukee Braves, who hit Dodger pitching like he owned it, especially, it seemed, in Ebbets Field. On July 31, 1954, Adcock had one of the greatest single days of hitting by any player in history when he borrowed a bat used by the Braves' backup catcher, Charlie White, and hit four homers and a double off four different Dodger pitchers for 18 total bases. (That record stood until 2002 when the Dodgers' Shawn Green broke it with 19 total bases in a game against the Milwaukee Brewers.)

The next day, Adcock hit a double in his first at bat and we wondered if we were ever going to be able to get this guy out. In his next at bat, however, Clem Labine beaned him after Adcock had swung completely around on the first pitch thrown to him in an obvious effort to hit another home run, which would have been his sixth in three days against us. This sent Adcock to the ground in a heap. They had to carry him off the field on a stretcher and, in the meantime, a skirmish broke out, as might be expected. Later in the game, the Braves' Gene Conley brushed back Jackie Robinson with one pitch and hit Duke with another. I know Labine—who visited Adcock in the clubhouse afterward and apologized for hitting him— always insisted it wasn't deliberate and I'd have to believe him. If nothing else, he was very conscious of the fact that Adcock was creaming every pitch thrown to him that he could hit and Labine, like any pitcher would be doing in that situation, was probably trying to keep him honest.

A couple of years later, in a game against the Giants at County Stadium in Milwaukee, Adcock was involved in one of the wildest pitcher-hitter confrontations anyone ever saw. In Adcock's first at bat, Giants pitcher Ruben Gomez hit him on the wrist with a pitch. As Adcock went to first base, he exchanged a few choice words with Gomez and then charged the mound, apparently having decided he wanted a piece of Gomez. Gomez, for his part, threw the ball at Adcock before hightailing it for the Giants' clubhouse. It was one of the funnier sights anyone had ever seen, this terrified Gomez running off the mound into the dugout with the big hulking Adcock in pursuit. I can understand why Gomez might have been afraid of Adcock, who was six-foot-four and powerful. Gomez had a hot temper, too, and even though he managed to escape, he didn't let it go at that. A few minutes later, he returned waving an ice pick, but thought better of doing anything with it after the umpires confronted him.

I was involved in a similar incident when I was managing the Red Sox. We were playing the Baltimore Orioles one day and Dennis Martinez, who had a little bit of a mean streak himself, was pitching for them and hit my big first baseman, George "Boomer" Scott with a pitch. Well, Boomer got dumped head-over-teakettle and was crawling around in the dirt trying to pick himself up to go out and charge Martinez. Problem was, he couldn't seem to get up and kept stumbling around on the ground there. In the meantime, Martinez started running for his life and was all the way out in left field when Boomer finally was able to get to his feet. Meanwhile, Earl Weaver, the Orioles manager, ran out of the dugout and screamed at Boomer: "Leave him alone, Boomer! He didn't mean it! Honest, he didn't mean it!"

It's funny, though, how the tables seemed to have turned. Nowadays, it's the hitter who considers it a personal insult if a pitcher throws inside to him. Back when I played, incidents of batters charging the mound, like Adcock did with Gomez, were far less common than they are now. You would usually have to have two to three hitters knocked down in the game before someone would take that kind of action. I've never seen so many hitters so sensitive when somebody throws one close to them as there are today. It's all right if they're hitting .345 with 40 homers, but if someone throws one inside they give 'em the stare. Well, I don't want to sound like an old-timer here, but it's a fact that if in 1955 someone threw one inside on me and I stared back at the pitcher, the next one might well be behind my neck. So the best thing to do is to brush yourself off and get back in there and try and hit.

But there's no question today hitters are more comfortable than at any time in the history of baseball. The game is simply played differently.

I'll give you another example of how different it is. In 1960, I was playing for the Cubs and we had a pitcher, Don Cardwell, who got traded over to us early in the season from the Phillies. We were playing the Giants and Cardwell buried one in on Orlando Cepeda's wrists. Alvin Dark was managing the Giants and right after this happened, I saw him walk down to the end of the dugout and say something to Jack Sanford, who was the Giants pitcher that day. "Uh oh," I said, "something's gonna happen here."

Sanford had also pitched for the Phillies and when he was there, Cardwell happened to be his roommate. The next inning, Cardwell came up to bat and Sanford threw one over his head. The catcher threw the ball back to Sanford in such a manner as if to say: "That ain't good enough." Sure enough, if the next pitch wasn't right at the back of Cardwell's head. *Roommates!*

All of this comes back to the "turf war" between pitchers and hitters over home plate. The pitchers think they own the plate—and even more—and they take exception to hitters moving up on it to take away their turf. I would also have to say baseball has probably exacerbated the situation with its continual vacillating about the strike zone, which, in itself, has become a joke. Now they've adopted this Questec system with cameras in the ballparks to supposedly monitor whether the umpires are correctly calling strikes and balls. To be honest, I'm still not sure if they really have determined exactly what the strike zone is.

I'll tell you why. A couple of years ago in spring training, Jim McKean, an American League crew chief, came into the Yankee camp in Tampa and asked Joe Torre if he could talk to our players about the strike zone. Joe agreed, and as we're all sitting there, McKean starts explaining how, in the past, the umpires were given the leeway of calling a strike on pitches three baseball widths off the plate. Think about that. Do you know how far that is? Anyway, McKean continues on by saying the league officials have ordered that to be reduced to a baseball-and-a-half off the plate I'm listening to this and I'm saying, "What the hell is this guy talking about here? This is nuts!"

Finally, I couldn't take it any longer. I wasn't trying to be a wise guy or anything, but I jumped up and said: "I can't believe what I'm hearing here! What is the purpose of having a plate if you're gonna call strikes that *aren't on it?* If you're so insistent on giving the pitchers a wider zone, why don't you just increase the size of the plate? At least then the hitters would have an idea where the damn strike is and could adjust to a wider plate."

This "revision" of the strike zone McKean was trying to explain was, I'm sure, in reaction to the justifiable outrage over Eric Gregg's pitch-calling in Game Five of the 1997 National League Championship Series in which Livan Hernandez of the Florida Marlins struck out 15 Atlanta Braves—most of them on pitches a foot off the plate. Afterward, Gregg made some comments about how "they all know my strike zone" and "this is how I always call that pitch." As if that made it right. I don't think pitchers ought to be saying: "I'm glad I got this umpire behind the plate today."

But getting back to the age-old hostilities, I also think the designated hitter has changed the pitcher-versus-hitter dynamics entirely. I still can't understand how you can have one rule for one league but not in the other, although in view of the ever-changing strike zone, baseball seems to thrive on indecision. In the opinion of the hitters, one pitcher of recent times who immediately took advantage of being in the American League was Jaret Wright, who broke in with Cleveland in 1997 and seemed to have this attitude of "I'll show these guys. I'm gonna knock 'em all on their ass." Everyone was complaining about him and it finally got to the point in 1999 when the American League president, Gene Budig, had to call Wright in to talk to him about his comportment on the mound. I don't know why Wright felt he had to resort to that macho business because he had real good stuff.

I do know that in all my years as a manager, I never ordered a pitcher to throw at a hitter. I always felt that was the pitcher's prerogative and some guys, like Drysdale, will do it automatically out of a sense of duty while others just don't have it in them. I also felt that if you're my pitcher and I say, "Go out there and knock him down" and he doesn't come close, the other players aren't going to respect him. So I wouldn't ever want to put one of my pitchers in that situation. This is not to say I didn't have team meetings in which I'd say we've got to protect our hitters—and hope I'd made my point with the pitchers.

I remember one time when I was with the Dodgers and our manager, Charlie Dressen, had a team meeting about knockdowns. We had two pitchers, Carl Erskine and Johnny Podres, who threw almost identical fastballs, curves, and great change-ups. They said to Dressen: "We've got three great pitches, if that's not enough to get the job done, then we don't know what is." To that someone replied: "If you knock guys down like Mays it'll only make 'em a better hitter." That was when Pee Wee Reese jumped up and said: "That's a lot of bullshit!"

To be honest, I think most hitters, deep down, have a pretty good idea when it's deliberate. There are certain hitters that can't hit the inside pitch and that's why you pitch them inside. Drysdale often used to complain about today's pitchers not throwing inside enough. "They're intimidated," he said. "They throw the perfect Spalding Guide pitch and then wonder why they get hit."

But if you miss by a couple of inches, the hitters think you're throwing at them. Hitters are so comfortable today they don't expect anything to happen and so when it does, they don't know how to get out of the way. I believe this was definitely the case with Mike Piazza in July 2000 when he got beaned by Roger Clemens and suffered a concussion. Partly because it was a Yankee-Mets series with all the media attention involved, the incident turned into a circus. It didn't help that Fox Sports kept replaying it over and over all season long.

I only know that Piazza was hitting .583 against Clemens with 3 homers prior to that game. In other words, he had gotten pretty comfortable facing Roger, and everyone knows Roger didn't get to 300 wins allowing hitters to handle him like that. Anybody who's ever heard the baseball term "chin music" knows it applies to Clemens, above all, who made a career of pitching inside and knocking hitters off the plate. True, the pitch to Piazza was right at his head, but I will never believe that Clemens threw it with the intention of beaning him. When you throw high and tight, there is very little margin for error and, in my opinion, Piazza was leaning into the pitch and simply didn't know how to get out of the way of it.

This is also why I think there are so many more cases of hitters charging the mound today after getting knocked down. I believe there's a way to put a stop to this—or at least a way to keep it to a minimum. If a batter charges the mound, I would allow only the catcher and the four umpires to be allowed in that circle from pitcher's mound to the plate—all in the role of peacemakers. No one else should be allowed into that circle, and if somebody does go in, they'd be fined. One of these days someone is going to get hurt as a result of these knockdowns and hitters charging the mound. Guys start charging out of the dugout toward the two combatants on the mound and all of a sudden someone gets hit from behind. There are a lot of lunatics in this game. I ought to know. I was one of 'em.

My pal Leonard Coleman, who was president of the National League from 1994 until baseball eliminated the office in 1999, told me a couple of funny stories involving hearings he held as a result of discipline he'd handed out in these incidents.

In 1999, Coleman said, he'd levied a four-game suspension on Shawon Dunston, who was then playing for the St. Louis Cardinals, for charging the mound and tackling and punching Dodger pitcher Jamie Arnold after being hit by a pitch. Dunston naturally appealed, as all the players do today, and the hearing was conducted by telephone.

"After asking Shawon a few questions, I said to him, 'It looked to me you had injury intent on your mind,'" Leonard related, "to which Shawon replied: 'Well, Leonard, when you're going to the mound, you're going there to take care of business.' Now usually I take a day to sleep on things, but as soon as I hung up the phone, I called Gene Orza over at the Players Association and said: 'It's obvious, Gene, you didn't have your witness prepared very well.' Orza just sighed and said: 'Can you believe what he said? He's been in the game fifteen years. He ought to know better than that! Don't bother calling me tomorrow with your decision. I already know what it is.'

"On the other hand, Dennis Cook, who was pitching for Florida at the time, had what I felt was a novel approach when he came in to appeal the three-game suspension I'd given him for throwing at a hitter. Even though he hadn't been thrown out of the game, I'd looked at the tape and it was obvious to me his hitting of this guy was deliberate. So when I told him what I thought, Cook didn't offer any alibi. 'Yeah, I hit him on purpose,' he said. 'But you've got to understand, I was only protecting my own hitters. I want you to know that was a professional hit. I wasn't trying to injure him.' A *professional hit*. I'd never heard that term used in baseball, but I have to admit, it gave me a chuckle. I told Dennis his technique was so novel I was reducing his suspension by a game."

The problem, of course, is retaliation. A guy gets whacked with a pitch and he wants the pitcher to pay for it, except in the American League where the pitcher doesn't have to hit, there is no payback other than the hitter taking matters into his own hands. The dumbest solution baseball ever came up with to deal with these situations is the umpire's warning of the pitcher. I know umpiring is a tough job, but I don't believe in warnings. By issuing a warning, what are you saying to the pitcher? You're saying he threw at the hitter. Well, you don't need a warning.

There's nothing in the rule book that says an umpire can't throw a pitcher out of the game—immediately—if, in his mind, he believes that pitcher hit a batter deliberately. A perfect example of that was when Armando Benitez, who was then pitching for the Baltimore Orioles, whacked Tino Martinez right in the back with a fastball after giving up a 3-run homer to the previous hitter, Bernie Williams in a game at Yankee Stadium in May of 1998. The home plate umpire, Drew Coble, immediately threw Benitez out of the game, although players already had started running out onto the field for the start of what became one of the worst brawls I've ever seen in baseball.

The point is, Benitez's action was so obvious and Coble used his own discretion. The problem with a warning is that it handcuffs the other pitcher who didn't do anything. His hitter is the one who got knocked down by the other pitcher and he doesn't get a shot because the warning applies to both pitchers. It's nuts.

There wasn't a person in the ballpark that Saturday of the Game Three Yankees–Red Sox ALCS who didn't think Pedro hit Garcia on purpose after the Matsui game-tying double. As such, the umpires should have thrown Pedro out of the game right there. No warning was necessary. I only wish they had. It would have saved me a whole of lot embarrassment.

# CHAPTER 3

# The Business of Baseball: Brains and Bosses

**W**hen I look back at it now, I'm really sort of amazed at the incredible success the Yankees had in the eight years I served as Joe Torre's bench coach. I say this because I don't know if there was ever a time the entire organization was on the same page as far as philosophy and even regarding a lot of the player evaluations. The latter isn't quite so important simply because I believe there's nothing wrong with having differing opinions within the organization on players. Nobody can be right all the time about a player, and when it comes to an evaluation process, a lot of times someone might offer an opinion or some firsthand information that the rest of the people weren't aware of. But when it comes to philosophy—a way of doing things—you need to have everyone working together for a common goal. I'd say that existed at the major league level with the Yankees between the general managers, (be it Bob Watson or Brian Cashman) and Joe who, in turn, filtered everything down to the coaches. But there were always a lot of others who were never around the major league club whose voices and opinions too often got heard the most, and that really bothered me.

I guess you could say it kind of all came to a head in my "mouse that roared" outburst in May of 2003.

With the George Steinbrenner Yankees, there always seemed to be these two factions—the major league staff and the group in Tampa in charge of the minor league operation. The papers in New York frequently described this as the "dysfunctional" Yankees. This is a word I was never familiar with before I came to the Yankees, but if it means what it sounds like, I would have to agree it fits. In all the places I've worked in baseball, I never saw anything like the "division of influence" that exists with the Yankees.

Although I was aware of this division my first couple of years as bench coach, I ignored it for the most part because we started winning right from the get-go in 1996, and Steinbrenner pretty much stayed out of Joe's hair and trusted his judgments on most everything. It was after the 1998 season—in which we had about the most perfect year a team could ever imagine, winning a record 125 games all told—that I began to see first-hand the little regard Steinbrenner held for the coaches.

It was early in the spring of 1999 that Joe got sick with cancer and

I had to take over as manager for him. I was hobbling around on a bad knee myself—bad enough that I was using crutches, going from field to field in spring training on a golf cart. I managed the team for nearly five weeks of spring training and then another five weeks of the regular season, during which Steinbrenner and I had our first public spat over the Hideki Irabu situation.

This was in April when Irabu, having been called a "fat toad" by Steinbrenner after failing to cover first base in his last start of the spring, told me he didn't want to pitch when the team opened the season on the West Coast. I couldn't believe this guy was actually refusing to pitch. I made the statement to the writers that Ramiro Mendoza would be starting the game in Oakland that Irabu, as the fifth starter, would have had. But it soon filtered back that Steinbrenner wanted Irabu to start the game. Mendoza wound up pitching, hurling eight shutout innings, and I brought in Irabu to complete the shutout in the ninth, but it had been a very trying time for me. I was never comfortable managing the team for Joe. My knee was killing me—to the point where I seriously considered going home after Joe got back—and it was clear my little interim managing stint had caused my relationship with Steinbrenner to change.

Let me say right here, I'm not looking for any medals. I was asked to do a job and I did it. I guess, however, Steinbrenner didn't view it as any big deal or extra effort on my part. I say this simply because I was never given any extra compensation for managing. Nor was anything ever said to me about even an expense account. I took the coaches out to dinner on my own money. I never considered submitting an expense report or inquiring about additional pay for managing. I figured if those things were supposed to be part of the deal, someone would have told me and no one ever mentioned anything to me. In the meantime, we got into our first real beef over Irabu and Steinbrenner refused to talk to me the entire last month of my interim managing term.

But then, before Joe, Steinbrenner changed managers as regularly as most guys change their underwear, which gives you a pretty good idea as to what he's always thought of managers. Gene Michael, who managed twice for Steinbrenner, once told me a funny story about the second time he got fired, in 1982. Michael said he was really hurt after the second time because he enjoyed managing and thought he'd done a good job. He was considering leaving the organization so he might manage elsewhere when Steinbrenner came to him and urged him to take a front-office job. As he told it, Steinbrenner said: "Why do you want to manage and be second-guessed by me every day when you can come into the front office and be one of the second-guessers yourself?"

The only people apparently held lower in Steinbrenner's esteem than managers are coaches. Even though we saw the team every day and knew the players inside and out, we were never asked our opinions on anything after those first couple of years. Instead, it seemed as if we were practically viewed as the enemy, or at the very least outsiders. I remember one day in the middle of the 2003 season, right around the trading deadline, Paul O'Neill, who lives in Cincinnati and watched the Reds games on a regular basis, was talking to me about Kent Mercker, a left-handed reliever on the Reds staff.

"Mercker used to be an overhanded pitcher, but now he comes at you sidearm a lot," O'Neill said. "I sure wouldn't want to hit against him now. If they're looking for bullpen guys, this is a guy they should strongly consider."

Well, Paul O'Neill is someone whose opinions on players I respect. The only problem was, there was nothing I could do with the information he gave me. He would have been better off just giving it right to Steinbrenner, but he assumed by telling one of Joe's coaches, it was the same as giving it to the organization as a whole. (By the way, Mercker wound up being traded by Cincinnati to the Atlanta Braves and finished the season as one of the most unhittable relievers in the league with a 1.95 ERA and a .227 opponents' batting average.)

One of the last times the coaches were allowed to be part of a staff meeting when I was there was in February 1999. We were all in Tampa anyway for the start of spring training when Steinbrenner assembled everyone at Malio's steak house to discuss the proposed trade of "Boomer" Wells to the Blue Jays for Roger Clemens. Even though everyone was unanimously in favor of making the deal since Clemens was coming off another Cy Young season, Steinbrenner wanted everyone's opinion on the record. There was a lot of discussion about money and contracts, which I didn't pay much attention to, and there was also the issue of Clemens having turned down the Yankees two years earlier to go to Toronto. We all agreed there might be a period of adjustment for him since the New York fans had always regarded him as the enemy.

But even after Cashman informed us we'd be throwing two other players—reliever Graeme Lloyd and infielder Homer Bush—who'd helped us win the previous year, we all agreed that when you've got a chance to get a Roger Clemens you've got to go for it. I remember, though, as the roundtable discussion was going on, Gene Michael began to say something only to be cut off by Steinbrenner who said: "You shut up." That really made me uncomfortable. I felt bad for Michael, who didn't say anything. I will say this. Steinbrenner never talked to me like that, maybe because he knew I'd just get up and walk out of the room. This makes me wonder if, even though Stick's been a longtime key evaluator of talent in the front office and instrumental in a lot of the team's success, he hasn't found himself any less second-guessed than when he was Steinbrenner's manager.

Regarding differences of philosophy within the Yankees, I'm referring to the "separation of church and state" between the major league staff and the player development department in Tampa. In the eight years I was there, all we kept hearing was all these great players they had in their system, especially the pitchers. Yet every time we needed a pitcher at the major league level, they sent us someone who didn't come close to getting the job done. We heard nothing but great reviews from Tampa on kids like Ed Yarnall, Randy Keisler, Ben Ford, Ryan Bradley, Adrian (El Duquecito) Hernandez, Brandon Knight, and Jake Westbrook, to name just a few who unfortunately never lived up to those reviews. Joe never complained, even to us. He just played the hand he was dealt, and won anyway because we were fortunate to never be without our full quota of veteran, established starters for long periods of time. I wouldn't have complained either, except that I got fed up with Steinbrenner always giving Tampa the credit when we'd won, and Joe and the coaches the blame when we'd be in a losing streak. I understand that many of the core players of those championship teams—Bernie Williams, Derek Jeter, Andy Pettitte, Mariano Rivera, Jorge Posada—were homegrown. But, with the exception of Posada, who came to us to stay in 1997, and Alfonso Soriano, who arrived with a flair in 2001, the 1996–2003 Tampa operation's contributions to our success, from what I could tell, were minimal—especially when it came to pitching. You'd think they might have found an acorn *once* in awhile.

Probably the best example of what I'm talking about was the signing of the Cuban refugee third baseman Andy Morales during spring training of 2001—apparently sight unseen. They gave this guy $4 million then brought him into the minor league camp to have Clete Boyer work with him. I saw Clete a couple of weeks after he'd started working with Morales and asked him what he thought of the new bonus baby third baseman. "I can't believe they gave this guy $4 million," Clete told me. "He can't do nothin'." Well, it didn't take long for the organization to conclude Clete's assessment was right on and within a year, they'd released Morales, only after finding out he was even a lot older than what they'd been told. But let me ask you: Who's accountable for throwing away $4 million like that? From what I understand, there were a lot more Latin American free agents they signed for big money that turned out to be busts too. Did Steinbenner just not want to know that the people he was so quick to give the credit for the organization's success were wasting millions of dollars of his money on players who couldn't play?

Now, before I go any further here, I have to be upfront about my friendship with Billy Connors, who's one of Steinbrenner's chief advisers in the Tampa operation and also the man who's been touted as the minor league pitching guru. People have said to me: "How can you be friends with Billy Connors when he's the one in charge of all those pitchers they sent to you that never panned out, and he's the one who Steinbrenner is always propping up over Mel Stottlemyre?"

I know Billy was caught in the middle of a couple of slights by Steinbrenner at Mel—the time when Steinbrenner overruled Joe and sent Jose Contreras to Tampa to work with Billy in 2003 and another time when he sent Hideki Irabu to work with Billy and then had

Billy accompany him back to New York to oversee his bullpen sessions. But I will say right here that Billy Connors does not have a bad bone in his body. He was told to do things he didn't want to do. No doubt these things were a slap in the face to Mel, and Billy would tell me: "I'm embarrassed by this." My response to him was: "The man loves you, Billy. All you've got to do is tell him 'this is not right' and don't do it."

Billy just never could bring himself to do that. I wished he had because Mel is also one of my dearest friends and I thought it was awful the way Steinbrenner would bring Billy into New York and proclaim him as the guru. I'm thrilled to death for Billy the way Steinbrenner feels about him. Everybody in baseball would like to have a "man" and Billy's got a "man," but it's put him in a lot of awkward spots.

As for all the minor league pitchers who never panned out, I realize Billy was one of the more upfront voices from Tampa in singing their praises. But what was he supposed to do? These were the pitchers he was given and, from an organizational standpoint, it was his job to build them up. I do know he had nothing to do with drafting any of them. All the time I was there, I kept hearing how Lin Garrett, the vice president of scouting in Tampa, was the pitching expert. Yet, it was pointed out to me the Yankees have not drafted, developed, and delivered to the big leagues a quality starting pitcher since Andy Pettitte. For starting pitching, they have always had to go to other organizations. So much for Tampa.

Speaking of Pettitte, I wasn't all that surprised when he left the Yankees to go home to Houston as a free agent after the 2003 season. Andy's a great man, a good person, a family man, and a gentleman. Do you think he forgot three years earlier when Steinbrenner wanted to dump him? Did George ever call him and tell him what a great player he'd been for us? Wasn't it only a year earlier George saw fit to go to lunch with Boomer at some hamburger joint in Clearwater and romance him? (It later was revealed by Boomer in his book how he played Steinbrenner for all it was worth in that lunch negotiation.) Why didn't George make any such effort to keep Pettitte, who, I think everyone would agree, was a much more true Yankee than Boomer? Why didn't George call Pettitte and say: "Let's get this thing straightened out"? I'm sure Andy Pettitte asked all those same questions as he said "yes" to the Astros and "good-bye" to the Yankees, the team he'd grown up with. Andy Pettitte's got feelings too.

Once Andy signed with Houston, I immediately thought it wouldn't be long before he talked his buddy, Clemens, who also lived there, to join him. There was quite a furor in New York over Roger coming out of a brief retirement, but to me the man returned in all honesty. You have to understand how close these two guys are and doesn't a guy have the right to change his mind? I know when Roger announced he was retiring in 2003 I felt he could win 14 games if he pitched in 2004. This has been the man's life and now he was going to be able to keep doing it with all sorts of stipulations that he wouldn't have to make trips where he wasn't pitching, and so on. As baseball people, have we not seen guys play one to two more years than they should and make clowns of themselves? Roger Clemens isn't in that category.

Sometimes in our game you never know how good someone is until he isn't there anymore. It took me awhile to realize how tough Pettitte was. In a way he reminded me of Sandy Koufax in that he was quiet and businesslike and never sought attention. Andy's only fault was that he wanted to be perfect—kind of like Paul O'Neill was with his hitting—and he was always so hard on himself. But he had as much fire in him as any pitcher I've ever known. When I think of Andy Pettitte, I think of two games he pitched in the postseason that defined him: Game Five of the 1996 World Series when he pitched 8⅓ shutout innings against Atlanta to give us a 3–2 series lead, and the 7⅔ shutout innings he threw against the A's in Game Two of the 2000 Division Series. I wonder when the Yankees will ever draft and develop another pitcher like Pettitte.

Steinbrenner is cheating himself when he thinks his people in Tampa know more about his club and other major league teams than his manager and his coaches. It's common sense to have had us in that room and hear our side of things too. He might not have heard what he wanted, but what did he have to lose? He just wants to hear what he wants to hear. You want to respect him for wanting to win every year, but does it ever occur to him the manager, coaches, and players want to win every year too? It's not that easy.

The way he is, I sometimes wondered if he was happier when we lost so he could start blaming people again. An example of what I mean is what happened after we beat the Red Sox in the ALCS in 2003. That was maybe the most satisfying victory I ever had in all my years in baseball, including all the World Series wins. It had been such an emotional and nerve-wracking series. I think everybody in New York was spent when it was over. And yet, where was Steinbrenner? Why didn't he come down to the clubhouse to congratulate Joe and the players? He'd been to the clubhouse all the other times we'd won a League Championship or a World Series. It was my thinking he'd made enough comments and treated enough people like dogs that he didn't want to show up. The only conclusion anyone could draw from this is that he just didn't like us. Why, I'll never know. All we ever did was win four World Championships and six American League pennants in eight years for him.

Of all the baseball bosses I've worked for or known in my fifty-six years in the game, Steinbrenner certainly was the hardest to figure out. I'm just glad he wasn't the first. If he had been, I doubt I'd have ever developed the love for this game that I have.

That's why I guess I can thank Buzzie Bavasi, my very first boss in the big leagues, for making the game so much fun for me. I was signed by the Brooklyn Dodgers in 1949 when the legendary Branch Rickey was running the ball club, but by the time I got to the majors, he'd moved on to the Pittsburgh Pirates and Walter O'Malley had taken over as owner. Buzzie moved into the general manager's job and even though he was a hard bargainer when it came to negotiating your contract, he really was a pal to the players. He'd loan us racetrack money, buy us dinners, and genuinely looked out for us. To me, he was like a father and after I retired as a player, I managed for him in San Diego when he was running the Padres. That was my first managing job in the majors and, looking back on it now, I wonder how I ever got another one. We lost 190 games in two years, finishing last both times, and I'd have to say it was on merit.

Buzzie ran the Padres with a free hand because the original owner there, C. Arnholt Smith, apparently knew and cared little about baseball. Smith was a big civic leader in San Diego and bought the expansion team for the good of the city. I only know that in two years of managing there I never once met the man.

I'm not sure exactly what it was, but Buzzie took a liking to me and always kind of let me have my own way—even to the point of giving me a preference of teams when he finally traded me from the

Dodgers in 1960. Of course, back then the owners and general managers had the upper hand. They paid the players what they wanted to pay them and traded them at will. There was no free agency, salary arbitration, or no-trade clauses. I remember in 1958, after I'd had my best season in the majors, hitting .262 with 17 homers and 60 RBIs, Buzzie gave me an $8,000 raise for 1959. I felt like a millionaire!

When it came to contract negotiations, Buzzie was definitely old school. He operated his whole career like he was protecting the owner's money—even when he went to the California Angels and worked for Gene Autry, the richest owner in the history of baseball who didn't care what he spent on players. Buzzie always said the biggest mistake he ever made in baseball was refusing to make Nolan Ryan the first $1 million ballplayer after the 1979 season. He just couldn't bring himself to be the one who crossed that historic salary threshold and Ryan, who loved the Cowboy, jumped ship to the Houston Astros. He then made Buzzie look bad by winning another 157 games in his career en route to the Hall of Fame.

It was all different then, though, and a lot of the owners—not Autry—were pure baseball people without the means to operate the way clubs do today. Their ballclubs were their businesses and the gains made by the players after the union came in drove all those owners out.

One such owner was Calvin Griffith, who ran the Minnesota Twins. I never worked for Griffith, but I knew him well and liked him a lot. The Twins were his livelihood, and after the games, you could go into the pressroom at old Metropolitan Stadium, where they played, and Griffith would be in there with his front office people having drinks. He loved sitting around talking baseball. I felt bad for him when free agency began to catch up to him and he couldn't afford to keep his best players. He took a beating from the press in Minnesota when he let players like Rod Carew, Lyman Bostock, Mike Marshall, and Ken Landreaux go. But he never seemed to let it bother him, always referring to himself as this "old baseball dinosaur" and he took pride in saying his team always paid its bills.

I think it's kind of interesting that, all these years after Griffith sold the Twins to the billionaire banker Carl Pohlad, they still can't seem to keep their best players. After losing to us with an overachieving, low-payroll team in the first round of the 2003 playoffs, they lost their two best bullpen guys, LaTroy Hawkins and Eddie Guardado to free agency.

Bill Veeck was another owner like Griffith whose sole source of income was derived from his baseball teams. I didn't know Veeck, since he operated only in the American League when I spent most of playing career in the National League. But in the 1970s, when he bought the Chicago White Sox for the second time, I was managing the Red Sox and the trips into Comiskey Park were always entertaining.

Veeck was the master showman with his exploding scoreboard and wacky promotions and I'd have loved to work for him. I can just imagine what he would have thought of my caper with the army helmet after I got beaned by that foul ball from Chuck Knoblauch in the Yankee dugout! (A little aside here on that: Since my wearing of the helmet in the dugout the next day was the result of a dare by Steinbrenner, the Yankees made a big deal of erecting a safety fence in front of the dugout the next year. They even put a cute little commemorative plaque on it that said "Don Zimmer Fence Company." The fence is still there but somebody—I have no idea who—had the plaque removed before the 2003 season.)

Although I never took part in them, the writers used to tell me about the all-night bull sessions Veeck would conduct in the Bard's Room (which was the press dining room) of Comiskey Park after games. He was just like Griffith in that he loved talking baseball. The only difference was he'd do it all night, drinking beer after beer, and nobody could ever outlast him. Veeck had a wooden leg, the result of his injuries in World War II, and the writers all swore it had to be hollow for him to be able to consume all that beer.

Autry, who owned the Angels from their birth as a franchise in 1961 until he died in 1998, was also a very special person I never got the privilege of working for. He loved baseball and he loved his players. He was a lot like Tom Yawkey, the owner of the Red Sox when I coached and managed for them from 1974 to 1980. Neither Autry nor Yawkey ever got to savor a World Series championship, but it wasn't for a lack of spending money. Yawkey made a career of buying the best players from the downtrodden, cash-strapped teams in the American League. In the 1930s, when he first took over the Red Sox, he bought future Hall of Famers Jimmie Foxx and Lefty Grove from Connie Mack's Philadelphia A's and in the 1940s he bought the St. Louis Browns' three best players, shortstop Vern Stephens and pitchers Ellis Kinder and Jack Kramer. Autry, on the other hand, was an even bigger spender than Steinbrenner when free agency came full bloom in the 1970s and 1980s, spending millions on star-quality players like Don Baylor, Bobby Grich, Joe Rudi, and Reggie Jackson.

Unfortunately, for all of their spending, neither Yawkey nor Autry ever won a world championship and, in Autry's case, he never even got to host a World Series. In a way, I guess, they were the standard-bearers of the old baseball saying, "you can't buy a pennant." On the other hand, if there was one thing I got really tired of hearing during my eight years with the Yankees when we were winning all those championships, it was all the stuff about the payroll.

I'll say this for Steinbrenner: The man wanted to win and he didn't care how much it cost him. The difference between him and Yawkey and Autry was that he obviously spent it on the right players. For that, you have to give credit to his baseball people at the major league level like Cashman and Michael who made those judgments. And I don't think you can say enough for Joe Torre, who molded all that talent into a team that never lost its focus on winning. Just because a ballplayer is making $5 million to $10 million per year, doesn't mean he's going to play up to that salary. Since we had the highest payroll, people kept writing and saying we were *supposed* to win. Well, it doesn't work that way, and I think even Steinbrenner—who also has almost always had the highest payroll and didn't win anything from 1982 to 1995—would have to agree that Joe Torre has seen to it he got the most for his money.

The one thing about Joe that stands out in my mind is that he's a people person. You've got to really be a jackass to get on his bad side, to the point where he'd actually take you on in public. With the Yankees, Joe has had a close working relationship with Cashman and, before that, Bob Watson, and I don't think you can underestimate the importance of this. When a general manager doesn't want to back the manager, what chance does that manager have?

A perfect example of what I'm talking about was the situation in Boston in 2000 when my pal, Jimy Williams, who was managing the Red Sox, got into a beef with his temperamental center fielder, Carl Everett. Everett had been nursing a hamstring injury and showed up late for a game in September, claiming he was unable to play. He later got into a clubhouse confrontation with Darren Lewis, the guy Jimy had replaced him with in center field. But when Jimy told the press he wasn't particularly pleased about a guy showing up late for a game with the team in a September pennant race, his boss, Red Sox GM Dan Duquette, made a counter statement about the only thing mattering was how Everett performed on the field. With that statement, Duquette completely undercut Jimy's authority.

Not that the general manager and the manager have to be pals, or even like each other. With the San Francisco Giants in the 1990s, it was common knowledge the general manager, Brian Sabean, and the manager, Dusty Baker, weren't crazy about each other. But Sabean, who's a real pro in my opinion, always supported Dusty—at least publicly—and, because of that, they were able to overcome their differences and be successful.

I wish that had been the case when I was with the Colorado Rockies in the mid 1990s. As bench coach for Don Baylor, I was caught in the middle of his simmering feud with Bob Gebhard, the GM. I talked to Don about trying to work things out with Gebhard for his own good, but ill feelings between the two of them had obviously become too deep-rooted. I wound up quitting in the middle of the 1995 season and Baylor managed to last three more years there, but I don't think it was ever a good situation, which was too bad. They're both good baseball men in my opinion.

I'm sure you can find exceptions to this, but if you look back at the most successful longterm baseball operations over the last fifty years, you'll find a close working relationship between the general manager and the manager. To cite just a few: The 1950s Yankees with GM George Weiss and Casey Stengel; the Dodgers from the 1950s to the 1970s with Buzzie and Walter Alston; the Baltimore Orioles with Earl Weaver and actually three GMs, Frank Cashen, Harry Dalton, and Hank Peters; and, most recently, the Atlanta Braves with GM John Schuerholz and his manager, Bobby Cox.

I was fortunate that in all of my managerial jobs, I had a GM who supported me—in San Diego with Buzzie, Texas with Eddie Robinson, Boston with Dick O'Connell and Haywood Sullivan, and the Chicago Cubs with my lifelong friend Jim Frey. I couldn't win in San Diego, but Buzzie's support gave me the confidence that I really could manage. My Texas experience was only slightly better, but I chalked that up to the fact that we had a goofy owner there in the old oilman, Eddie Chiles, who fired Robinson in the middle of the 1982 season and told me I essentially had the final word on all personnel decisions, before firing me as well twelve days later.

My firing in Boston was heartbreaking—not for me but for the guy who did it, Haywood Sullivan. The team wasn't playing well and Sully came down to my office to deliver the bad news to me, but just couldn't bring himself to do it. I finally had to console *him* and told him I understood and that it wasn't going to affect our friendship, which it didn't.

When Frey hired me to manage the Cubs in 1988, a lot was made about the fact that we'd gone to high school together. We pretty much put that to rest when the Cubs won the NL East in 1989. And when I was ultimately fired there two years later, it wasn't Frey who did it, but rather Don Grenesko, an appointed executive from the *Chicago Tribune* who didn't know anything about baseball. I loved managing in Chicago—it's one of the great baseball towns—but I had no regrets about being fired there simply because the guy who fired me wasn't a baseball man. For some reason, the Tribune Company, which owns the team, felt it had to put one of its corporate guys in charge of the baseball club, and the results were predictable for many years after Frey and I left. I'd like to believe it's no coincidence the Cubs have been a much more successful operation with Andy MacPhail—who comes from a family of Hall of Fame baseball people—as team president instead of someone with no baseball background like Grenesko.

What can I say? I'm a baseball man. It's all I've ever known. Maybe if I hadn't grown up in an organization like the Dodgers where the owner, the general manager, and the manager were always on the same page, I might not feel the way I do about how an organization ought to run. Overall, I'd have to say I've been pretty spoiled, working as I did for such great organizations, and now I've come full cycle, getting hired by the Tampa Bay Devil Rays right here in my hometown. Someday, I hope to be able to tell you how, behind every great organization, there's a senior adviser. Once, that is, they figure out just exactly what a senior adviser is.

# CHAPTER
## 4

**Pal Joe**

The best thing for me about being in baseball so long and working in so many cities is the many friends I've made. It's been kind of like one of those pyramid schemes where, in each succeeding place, you meet twenty to thirty more people who get added to your roster of friends and before you know it, the number is in the thousands.

I knew Joe Torre casually prior to 1996, having managed against him in the National League when I was with the San Diego Padres and he was then a superb-hitting third baseman with the St. Louis Cardinals. I've always liked telling the story about how Joe, unintentionally, embarrassed me one day by beating the Padres with what should have been a ground ball out. Instead, unfortunately, it got booted by my second baseman. It was during the 1971 season in which Torre wound up being named National League Most Valuable Player by leading the league in hitting (.363), hits (230), RBI (137), and total bases (353).

He had certainly made his presence known and in a conversation earlier in the year I'd told my general manager, Buzzie Bavasi, that if there was one guy in the league I would never let beat me, it was Joe Torre. Anyway, I found myself in a position to live up to that promise when Torre came to the plate in the ninth inning of a game we were winning by a run, with runners at second and third. But instead of walking him intentionally to the empty base, I chose to pitch to him and he hit a grounder to my second baseman Derrel Thomas, who kicked the ball all the way into the right field corner as both runners scored and we lost. Afterward, Buzzie couldn't resist tweaking me: "I thought you said you'd never let Torre beat you!"

That was really the extent of my relationship with Torre—a distant respect—and though our paths crossed again in the late 1980s and early 1990s when he was managing the Cardinals and I was managing the Chicago Cubs, we'd exchange small talk but that was about it. So you can imagine my surprise to get that call from him in early November 1995, asking me if I'd like to end my retirement and join on with him as his bench coach for the Yankees. It was during the postseason that Buddy Bell, who was still a coach with Cleveland, called me to say that he was expecting to be named manager of the Tigers and would I be interested in being his bench coach? I told him that was too far down the line to make a commitment at that time. Then a couple of weeks after the World Series I got the unexpected call, and going back to the Yankees and New York, however, was something else.

Even though, as I said, I didn't really know Joe that well, I suspected he was going to be very easy to work with, and I realized I was right about that right from the get-go. One of the first days of spring training in 1996 I went into his office and said: "I'm not a laid-back guy. If I have something to say, I will, and if you ask me questions, I'll answer 'em as if I was managing the team. I will say four to five things to you and if you don't choose to use any of 'em, don't worry about hurting my feelings." Joe just smiled and said: "That's exactly what I want you to do."

About two weeks into spring training, I remember going home and telling my wife, Soot: "This is really gonna work." That's how sure I was. We just hit it off right away and everything was positive, especially from his part.

As that spring wore on, I watched the club play and toward the end of camp I said to Joe: "This is not a typical Yankee team with a lot of power. I think we might have to do some of the little things to manufacture some runs." You don't want to do these things in spring training against the teams you're going to play during the regular season, but once the season began, we started putting in a running game. For instance, I knew from having had him in Chicago, that Joe Girardi had some speed for a catcher and was also very adept at bunting. He was on first base one day and I said to Joe: "Girardi can steal second on this guy."

Joe looked at me and said: "Are you sure? This guy's a catcher."

"I know that," I replied, "but I had this guy in Chicago and I ran him a lot."

Well, I think Girardi might have set a record for steals by a catcher in 1996 with 13 in 17 attempts.

It was sometime during that season Joe made a statement that he was not the gambler I was. Joe was every bit the boss, but he bought into a lot of things I suggested about our running game. I never suggested anything to him where people could hear me because he had to manage the team. It got to a point where he'd needle me all the time. The count would be 1-1 on the batter and he'd say to me: "If it's a ball, play hit and run?"

"Cute," I'd say.

One day, Girardi got thrown out by a foot trying to steal and I said to Joe: "Where the hell was *he* going?"

Joe laughed and said: "He's obviously been listening to you too long."

We kept the running game going pretty good over the first few months of the season and soon the media was saying we were playing National League baseball. They cited the fact that both Joe and I had National League roots, but that had nothing to do with it. Joe simply managed the team according to his personnel. Then, late in the season we got "Big Daddy" Cecil Fielder and Darryl Strawberry and suddenly the Yankees took on a more conventional look with a power game. We no longer needed to run as much. I remember one time, though, when Big Daddy was on third base and Tino Martinez was on first—our two slowest runners. I turned to Joe and said: "What do you think about a double steal here?"

"Now I know you're really a whacko," he said.

"I don't know," I replied, "I just thought we might need to remind everyone that we still have a running game here."

Needless to say, Joe and I got real close real quick. We'd hang out together before and after games and I, of course, got blamed for taking Joe to the racetrack. It was as if I corrupted him, but the fact is one of the first times I ever met him was at Derby Lane in St. Pete thirty years ago when he was there playing the dogs with his brother Frank. Early on in 1996, Joe would ask me if I was going to the track and I'd say: "Yeah, I'm going, but I don't need no help."

On one of our first road trips to Baltimore, he said: "Where are you going?" and I replied: "I'm going to Pimlico." He said: "Great, I'll go with you."

We get out to the track where the horses are running live and we get a table in the dining room to have lunch. There's a television above us, and a little card on the table that has numbers 32 for Calder and 21 for Philadelphia, 18 for Belmont and so on. This was all new to Joe and I've got him clicking all the channels because I've got bets at all these other tracks. He says to me: "You've got me crazy here! Managing's a lot easier than this!"

Another time I was going to the track and Joe handed me $200 and said: "Bet for me."

I don't like doing that unless I know what I'm betting, but I did it anyway and brought him back $400. A week later, we did the same thing and this time I brought him back $800. Then he said to me: "How easy is *this?*" After that, he started going with me.

If there are three things Joe enjoys most off the field it's the best cigars, the best wines, and the best restaurants. When we left spring training in 1996, we opened the season in Cleveland and Joe took all the coaches to this exclusive Italian restaurant where he naturally

knew the owner. We're sitting around the table and Joe orders a bottle of red wine, which gives me a headache.

The waiter brings over the bottle, opens it up, and hands the cork
to Joe. Joe gives a little sniff of the cork and waits while the waiter
poured a little splash of the wine into his glass. Now you've got to
remember, I'm just a guy from Sedamsville, a shot-and-a-beer suburb
of Cincinnati. So I'm watching closely as Joe picks the glass, holds it
up in the air, and starts twirling it around. Finally, this got to be too
much for me.

"What is all this shit about?" I asked.

"I'm looking for the legs," Joe replied.

"The *legs? What* legs? What the hell are you talking about?"

Well now they're all laughing as Joe finally gets to actually taking
a drink of the wine and says to the waiter: "Ah, yes, bring it on."

Well, I don't say anything else until the next time we go out to
dinner and Joe starts in on this same ritual.

"Are we looking for the damn legs again?" I asked.

"You betcha," Joe replied.

From that day on, every time we went out to a restaurant for dinner with Joe, they'd give me my little glass and I would put on the
act. I'd wait for the waiter to pour me a splash of the wine, then I'd
swish it around and hold it up into the light, and say to him: "Okay,
let's see if I can find some legs now!"

Joe would always tell me he was just trying to give me some culture.

Joe's got friends who own restaurants in every city in America. All
he has to do is call and they'll stay open for him. Ever since Joe got
sick with his prostate cancer he's become fanatical about his diet
and they'll all cook his food precisely the way he requests it.

A lot of times when he'd take the coaches out, he'd bring along David Szen, the traveling secretary, and after dinner we'd all play "liars poker" with dollar bills. The restaurants invariably put us in a private room and we had some of the funniest times with those games.

In the eight years I spent with Joe, I very seldom saw him get really angry. He didn't let too many things bother him, especially after he went through the cancer thing. One time, though, we were sitting in his office and the phone rings. It was the first time Joe had started to get a little bad press and the caller on the other end was his sister, the nun. She'd apparently been listening to one of those talk radio shows and she's all upset about her brother getting this bad publicity. I'm sitting there as this conversation is going on and I can see Joe is getting annoyed. Finally he cuts her off and says. "Then just don't bother to read the papers or listen to those shows!" As far as I know, he never read the papers either.

Joe's a very confident guy, and that rubs off on his players. He never shows worry or concern. I think back to that meeting he had with Steinbrenner after we got clobbered 12–1 at home by the Braves in the first game of the 1996 World Series. Steinbrenner was pacing around the room and grumbled about how badly we played, all but throwing in the towel. Joe just let him vent and then said: "Boss, we may get beat tomorrow too, but then we're going to Atlanta, which is my town, and we'll sweep them there and come home and wrap it up here." Steinbrenner just shook his head, but as history has recorded, that's exactly what happened.

My favorite moment of that World Series, which pretty much sums up the relationship Joe and I had, was the tenth inning of the pivotal fourth game. We'd come all the way back from the 6–0 deficit Kenny Rogers had put us in after three innings, and now in the tenth, we had pushed across a couple of go-ahead runs. In the process, however, Joe had used up everyone on the bench and we didn't have anyone to play first base in the bottom of the inning. That was when Charlie Hayes, our third baseman, came over to Joe and volunteered to play first. Joe looked at me and I just shrugged. Hayes claimed he'd played first a couple of times in the past and, being as we didn't have anyone else anyway, Joe said: "Go to it." Then he turned to me and laughed: "We do things by the seat of our pants around here, don't we?"

You can see why guys loved playing for him. Players all have insecurities, even the best of them, and they look to the manager for confidence. I think the confidence that Joe always displayed was a factor in Steinbrenner staying away from him and not coming down on the players in the papers like he'd always done before. On the occasions they did have a meeting of the minds, Joe wasn't afraid to speak his to Steinbrenner.

I remember one time after we'd lost a game and Steinbrenner had a meeting and said: "I'd have these guys out there running their asses off." To that Joe replied: "George, I don't know how many times I've got to tell you, this is baseball, not football."

A funny incident involving Steinbrenner and Joe happened in a game we were playing the Red Sox during the regular season in 2002. Mike Cubbage, then the Red Sox third base coach, is a diabetic and, because of that, he wears this little pouch on his belt that enables him to inject insulin at a moment's notice if necessary. Anyway, it was sometime in the middle of the game when we got word in the dugout that Steinbrenner, who was watching on TV in Tampa, had spotted Cubbage's pouch and was demanding to know what it was.

He was ordering it to be checked while apparently insinuating it was a cell phone! We had a good laugh about that, and Lou Piniella told me a similar story about when he was managing the Yankees in the 1980s.

As Lou told it, the Yankees were beating the Angels 2–0 and Tommy John was pitching for the Yankees against Don Sutton. Both of them had reputations for doctoring the ball. After Sutton came in from the mound one inning, the TV cameras caught him removing something from his pocket. The dugout phone immediately started ringing and when Lou picked it up, it was Steinbrenner on the other end, screaming about Sutton cheating.

"He's saying to me, 'Sutton's cheating and you're not doing anything about it!'" Piniella related. "So I let him go on and then I calmly asked him: 'George, what's the score?' He says, 'It's 2–0, what difference does that make?'

" 'The difference, George,' " Piniella said, " 'is that our pitcher is cheating better than their pitcher.' "

I always felt Joe was a master at handling Steinbrenner. He was careful about picking his battles with him. For the first few years I was there, Joe, Mel Stottlemyre, another coach, and I would always play cribbage in Joe's office after batting practice. It was never for money, just for fun, and it was a great form of relaxation before the games. We never bothered anybody. Then one day, Steinbrenner came in and saw us playing and made a comment about the card games. He put the word out he didn't want any more card games in the clubhouse before games. Joe could have defied him, but that's not the kind of person he is.

It was the same thing with the platform we had behind the batting cage. One spring training when Joe had a bad knee, he mentioned to someone about how taxing it was to stand behind the cage for so long while he was watching the hitters hit. The next day, the grounds crew erected this stand behind the cage where Joe could sit and observe the whole field during the workouts. I would often sit up there with him and even Steinbrenner would come out on occasion and sit there. It was such a good idea, they had another stand built in New York for our home games at the Stadium.

Then one day in June of 2002, Juan Rivera, one of our young outfielders, was shagging flies during pregame drills and crashed into a cart that had been left in foul territory by the grounds crew. Lee Mazzilli was the coach hitting the flies to Rivera and, because of that, he was the one Steinbrenner blamed for the accident. I don't know if Steinbrenner ever talked to Mazzilli again after the incident. But a side effect of the mishap was that, the next day, the platform behind the batting cage was suddenly gone, never to return. Only a cynic would suggest Steinbrenner had it removed as a means of punishment for Joe and the coaches.

I think another measure of the kind of guy Joe Torre is would be the ease he has in working with people. When Joe was hired by the Yankees he was told he could bring in three coaches: a bench coach, a hitting coach, and an outfield coach. Mel had already been hired as the pitching coach, Willie Randolph was a fixture as the third base coach, and Tony Cloninger was a holdover as the bullpen coach. As I said before, he hired me, without really knowing me, as bench coach, and brought in Chris Chambliss and Jose Cardenal, who both had worked for him in St. Louis, as the hitting coach and outfield coach, respectively. I don't know of any staff that worked better together, especially Joe and Mel. Ordinarily, a manager especially wants to pick his own pitching coach because that's the one relationship he has to be completely in tune with on the staff. With Joe and Mel, it was as if they'd worked together their entire lives, and it was not at all surprising to me that Mel decided to come back for Joe's final year of his contract in 2004.

But through the eight years there were a number of changes on the staff—we went through two more batting coaches after Chambliss—and Joe had no problem with any of the new coaches the organization brought in. The only coach I believe he had a direct hand in hiring was Mazzilli, who, with Joe's blessing, was originally hired by the organization as a minor league manager in 1997 and moved up to the big league staff in 2000 when Cardenal left. I know Maz considers Joe to be his mentor. The reason I bring this all up is because I have always been a firm believer in the manager picking all his coaches. I've never understood why organizations will hire a new manager—supposedly because they want to change the team philosophy—and then not let him name any of his coaches.

This happened twice after the 2003 season—both times involving first-time managers. In Chicago, the White Sox hired Ozzie Guillen, a big fan favorite there who'd never managed anywhere, and in Baltimore, the Orioles hired Mazzilli, who had the three years of minor league managing experience with the Yankees. Because both of them were grateful to get their first big league managing jobs, they didn't make any waves about the organization telling them who their coaches were going to be. Still, wouldn't you think if you're hiring a rookie manager you'd want to give him every comfort? In Mazzilli's case, two of the guys on his staff, Sam Perlozzo and Rick Dempsey, had both interviewed for the manager's job themselves. They're both professionals and Maz, being a lot like Joe, won't have any problem working with all new people, but it's human nature for the other coaches to be disappointed over not getting the job.

One of the first times I remember this happening was in 1990 when the White Sox hired Jeff Torborg as their manager and told him he could bring in only one coach, Dave LaRoche, the former pitcher he'd worked with when he was coaching for the Yankees. The White Sox general manager at the time, Larry Himes, said: "We'll decide who the coaches are going to be." I remember thinking to myself: "That's a helluva endorsement for Torborg."

I should make the point here that I was not the only one to make suggestions to Joe. He let all the coaches make suggestions and they could feel comfortable doing that because he would listen to them. I know for a fact you can't say that about a lot of managers. One of the best feelings I've ever had was when I'd make a suggestion and it would work out, Joe would tap me on the leg with his fist. That made me feel like we were a real team.

I've said many times no one will truly appreciate how much Joe Torre has meant to the Yankees until he's gone. A big part of the team's success, if you ask me, has been Joe's inner strength, which is one of the reasons the owner, for the most part, has steered clear of him. Whenever Steinbrenner would come into Joe's office after a tough loss or when we were playing bad it was to vent. Not at Joe, but at the circumstances. To the best of my knowledge, he never dared to second-guess or criticize Joe to his face, even though he'd be constantly doing that with anyone and everyone up there in his private box. With all the other managers Steinbrenner had, he wouldn't hesitate to pick up the phone and berate them, as he does with everybody in the organization.

I remember once in 1983 when I was third base coach for Billy

The 1955 Brooklyn Dodgers.
*(Photo by Barney Stein. Courtesy Don Zimmer Collection)*

Celebrating in the dressing room after their ninth straight victory
over the Phillies on April 21, 1955, are Brooklyn Dodgers Gil Hodges,
Don Zimmer, Jackie Robinson, Pee Wee Reese (top), and Carl Furillo.
*(Courtesy United Press Telephoto)*

Don Zimmer hits a grand-slam home run for the Dodgers,
driving in Walt Moryn, Duke Snider, and Don Hoak
on September 9, 1955, at Wrigley Field.
*(Courtesy Don Zimmer Collection)*

The Brooklyn Dodgers parade through their favorite borough.
*(Courtesy Diamond Images)*

Dodgers Don Zimmer, Don Hoak, and Clem Labine.
*(Courtesy Diamond Images)*

Don Zimmer, with Jerry Lewis,
working out with the Chicago Cubs in 1960.
*(Courtesy Don Zimmer Collection)*

Don Zimmer with Ted Williams in the summer of 1976 at Fenway Park.
*(Courtesy Don Zimmer Collection)*

Yogi Berra, President Gerald Ford, Tommy Lasorda, Don Zimmer,
and Joe Garagiola in January 1978.

*(Courtesy Don Zimmer Collection)*

Bear Bryant with Don Zimmer in the summer of 1978.
*(Courtesy Don Zimmer Collection)*

Earl Weaver with Don
Zimmer in the late 1970s.
*(Courtesy Don Zimmer Collection)*

Paul Newman with Don Zimmer in July 1992.
*(Courtesy Don Zimmer Collection)*

Oil painting presented by the New York Yankee players to Don Zimmer
in 1998 to commemorate his first fifty years in professional baseball.

*(Courtesy Don Zimmer Collection)*

Sign posted at Yankee Stadium after Don was hit by a foul ball off Chuck Knoblauch's bat during a game on October 5, 1999. *(Courtesy Don Zimmer Collection)*

Don Zimmer with President George W. Bush in the Oval Office in May 2001.
*(Courtesy Don Zimmer Collection)*

Don and Soot Zimmer's fiftieth-anniversary party
on August 16, 2001. From left to right in the back row are:
Lane, Marian, and Tom Zimmer; Whitney and David Mollica;
Ron and Beau Zimmer; and Donna Zimmer Mollica.

*(Courtesy Don Zimmer Collection)*

Don Zimmer at the dedication of "Don Zimmer Field"
at Griffin Park in Windham, New Hampshire, with Rico Petrocelli,
Mel Stottlemyre, and Joe Torre.
*(Courtesy Don Zimmer Collection)*

Soot Zimmer at the
"Don Zimmer Field" and
monument, August 2002.
*(Courtesy Don Zimmer Collection)*

Don Zimmer being thrown to the ground by the Boston Red Sox's
Pedro Martinez after Roger Clemens threw a high ball to Manny Ramirez in
the fourth inning of Game Three of the American League Championship
Series, October 11, 2003, at Fenway Park in Boston.

*(Newark* Star-Ledger *photo by Chris Faytok, via AP)*

Lou Piniella talks with Don Zimmer during the Tampa Bay Devil Rays'
first workout of the season on March 15, 2004.

*(Photo courtesy Al Behrman/AP)*

Martin, we'd lost a game and Billy was talking to the writers in his office only to be interrupted by the ringing of the phone on his desk. On the other end was Steinbrenner who was screaming so loud at Billy all the writers could hear everything he was saying. A few minutes after the room cleared out, I walked in and found Billy sitting at his desk, sobbing. He was so embarrassed at being dressed down like that in front of the writers and all I could do was to put my arms around him in an effort to console him.

Another reason I think Steinbrenner laid off Joe was because he realized the hold Joe had over his players. In the eight years I was there, I can think of only two players, Ruben Sierra and Raul Mondesi, who had any sort of public spats with Joe. And in Sierra's case, four years in baseball purgatory after being cut loose by the Yankees made him a changed man. It may be remembered, during the 1996 season, Sierra got on Joe's very short "bad" list by calling him a liar. It was the age-old player-manager dispute over playing time and Sierra told the press that Joe had reneged on a promise to play him more in the outfield than at designated hitter. Then, after he was traded to Detroit on July 31 that year for Cecil Fielder, Sierra made some comment about being glad to be away from the Yankees because "all they care about over there is winning."

So it was only natural when we reacquired Sierra in a trade with Texas on June 6, 2003, that the press immediately brought up all that past ill will between him and Joe. There were some things written about how Sierra would upset the good chemistry that had existed in the Yankee clubhouse since 1996. What they didn't know was that this was a different Sierra from the one we had in 1996. Five releases in three years can humble a man and Sierra had to go all the way back to an independent league team in Atlantic City to resurrect his career. You've got to give him credit. He took stock of himself and worked hard to make it all the way back, if nothing else as a still-dangerous and productive hitter on a part-time basis.

In the first couple of weeks for us, Sierra hit solo homers on back-to-back days, got an eleventh-inning hit against the Mets, then hit a game-winning 3-run homer against the Orioles. It was around that time I went up to him and said: "You came back here in the right frame of mind and you've picked us up at a time when we needed picking up. Don't think this has gone unnoticed."

I know he appreciated that, and despite what was written, I know Joe felt Sierra was a different guy from the moment he arrived back. It is a measure of the regard Joe had for Sierra that the Yankees re-signed him for 2004 as an extra outfielder and pinch hitter. To me, to be a good pinch hitter you've got to get your cuts because you can't reduce yourself to only one strike. You've got to go up there swinging, and that's what Sierra does.

From what I was told, Joe's reconciliation with Sierra came full flower at the start of the 2004 season. In the first full squad meeting in spring training, Joe stood up as always and went through a long list of rules for the players. Then he called on Sierra, who, according to the other players, did a quick imitation of Joe's walk. Apparently, this is something Sierra had been doing a lot in front of the players in 2003, drawing lots of laughs. It was the same thing at the 2004 spring training meeting, and no one laughed harder than Joe.

"You talk so seriously throughout the meeting, it was good to laugh," Joe told the reporters. He went on to say that after the Yankees traded him in 1996, Ruben made it clear how upset he was.

"He spent this whole time trying to get back at me," Joe joked. "And this is the best he could come up with."

Mondesi, on the other hand, was, in 2003, a lot like Sierra in 1996. He couldn't adjust to Joe's team concept, and when he ultimately left, it was at Joe's insistence. It all started when Joe pinch-hit for him with Sierra in the eighth inning of a game against the Cleveland Indians, July 27 at Yankee Stadium. Mondesi was furious and let his feelings known to the press. Then, five days later, when we began a nine-game road trip in Boston, he was a no-show. Joe was justifiably furious. Mondesi had played hard, but he lost it with Joe when he made such a big deal about being pinch hit for. He should've known that Joe had pinch hit in the past for Paul O'Neill, Tino Martinez, and even future Hall of Famer Wade Boggs for goodness sakes! None of them liked it, but they understood and they knew that Joe would never embarrass a player. So on July 20, when the team was in Anaheim, it was announced Mondesi was traded to the Arizona Diamondbacks for backup outfielder David Delucci. As Brian Cashman said: "The Yankees and Mondesi are not going in the same direction. He's a player that plays hard, but I don't know if he's ultimately on the same page with us." Joe simply said: "It's unacceptable what he did to us."

Joe tried to be right with Mondesi. When Mondesi came to us from Toronto in July of 2002, there had been a lot of stuff in the papers about him being a problem player who never lived up to his ability. They also said this was Steinbrenner's deal, but that wasn't the case. Joe liked Mondesi's bat, and you had to like his arm in right field. I think we were kind of hoping he could have the same sort of career resurgence in New York as David Justice had a couple of years earlier when we brought him over from Cleveland. He gave us some spurts, but in the end it didn't work out, which was Mondesi's loss. When his career is over and he looks back on it, he'll probably realize how fair a manager Joe Torre was.

In that regard, Joe's biggest challenge was probably late in the 2000 season when the Yankees picked up Jose Canseco on waivers. Along with "Big Daddy" Fielder and Darryl Strawberry, that suddenly gave us three designated hitters—all of them with egos. Joe called each one of them into his office and explained to them the situation, saying: "I can't play all three of you, obviously, but I'll do the best I can to get everybody some at bats." Somehow, he did, too.

For the first six to seven years with the Yankees, Joe was never much for meetings, but toward the end of 2003 we seemed to have a lot of them, I think more out of superstition on Joe's part than anything else. It all started when he had a meeting before one game and Joe decided to ask Nick Johnson—who, if he says ten words during the course of a day, it's a lot—to get up and speak. Well, Nick stands up and starts searching for something to say, using a lot of "uh's" and "er's" and finally blurts out: "Let's just go out there and play hard!" Everybody laughed and we won that day, so Joe decided to do it again with Nick the next day. The same thing happened, Nick hemmed and hawed, trying to find the right words and then, with a sheepish grin, said: "Let's just go out there and play hard!"

At that point, Joe called up Hideki Matsui, who always had to use his translator. Joe said to the translator: "What does Hideki want to say?" The translator said something in Japanese to Matsui, who, in turn, said something in Japanese back to him. Then the translator turns to all the guys in the room and says: "Hideki says he feels the same as Nick!" Everybody cracked up, and I think Joe felt he'd come up with a novel way of keeping everybody loose, which is why we kept this ritual up.

You've heard the old Leo Durocher line about nice guys finishing last. Well, Joe Torre is one nice guy who did nothing but finish first for Steinbrenner. I've seen Joe get mad, and I've seen him chew out a player in his office, but he's always under control. If I had Joe's temperament, I'd still be a Yankee. But I'm not like him.

# CHAPTER
# 5

What Have
They Done
to My Game?

I 'm not exactly sure what qualifies a lifetime .235 hitter to speak with any kind of authority about the overall state of baseball, other than the fact that, to have lasted in the game for fifty-six years, I had to have learned something. More than anything, I guess, I learned how to survive on limited ability. At the same time, friends of mine have told me I remind them of that 120-year-old Indian in the movie *Little Big Man* who sits there and reflects on all the history he's lived through. I never saw the movie—I don't go the movies—

but I can certainly relate to that as far as my baseball experiences are concerned.

It was most definitely a very different game when I first came up to the Brooklyn Dodgers in 1954 as another in the long line of short-stop hopefuls who would never succeed in replacing Pee Wee Reese. Baseball had only sixteen teams then, none further west than the Mississippi River. The highest paid player in the game was Stan Musial at $80,000 and the average baseball salary, I think, was about $10,000. Obviously, this was some twelve years before the players became unionized under Marvin Miller and began making enormous gains in just about everything. Free agency, salary arbitration, no-trade clauses were things we'd never even dreamed about. Oddly enough, the only players who were making any real money from baseball in those days were the unproven amateurs right off the sandlots. They called them "bonus babies" and the one I remember most was Paul Pettit, a teenage left-handed pitcher from California who got $100,000 to sign with the Pittsburgh Pirates in 1950. He never made it, and neither did most of the other high school kids who signed for those huge bonuses back then—like Frank Leja, the first baseman the Yankees signed and billed as "the next Lou Gehrig." Leja played a total of 26 games in the majors, or 2,138 fewer than Gehrig. I will say this, though. It's no easier today scouting high school kids and trying to project what they'll be able to do four or five years later.

I'd have to say the biggest difference in the game today and the game when I played is the size of the players. Back in 1998 when the Yankees were putting together their greatest season in terms of wins, 125, people kept asking me to compare them to the 1955 Dodger team that I played on. It was simply not a comparison I could make, for this reason: Our shortstop on the 1955 Dodgers, Pee Wee Reese, was five-foot-nine, 175 pounds, and hit a total of 80 home runs in sixteen years in the big leagues. He's in the Hall of Fame, and deservedly so, but if he were playing today, he'd be dwarfed, literally, by the other shortstops in both size and offensive production. Our Yankee shortstop, Derek Jeter, by contrast, is six-foot-three, 195 pounds, and had 80 home runs by his fifth year in the majors. At the end of his career, you put his stats next to Pee Wee's and that's all you need to see as far as how the game has changed.

Players today are bigger, stronger, and more powerful and, at the same time, can run as fast or faster than the players of yesteryear. Even though they called me "Popeye" because I had muscles like the comic book sailor, I can assure you I never lifted a weight in my life. Can you imagine walking into Ebbets Field and seeing a weight room? We didn't have any places to work out and, so, when the season was over, we put our gloves and spikes away and didn't pick them up again until reporting to Vero Beach the following spring. We certainly couldn't afford to go to Florida in January, like so many of today's players do, to start working out.

I'll be honest. I was never big on weight lifting for baseball players—I always felt it was too easy to get hurt and that extra muscle wasn't necessarily a good thing in baseball. But one of the things I learned from Billy Martin when I coached for him was that, if your players tell you they believe in it, then, OK, let them lift weights but only in an organized situation. That's pretty much the way it is today with most players having their own personal trainers year round.

I know there are a lot of old-timers who grumble that today's players couldn't carry their jocks since they played in an era before expansion when there were only sixteen teams. That's a lot of hooey. Where couldn't Jeter, Alex Rodriguez, Barry Bonds, Roger Clemens, or Sammy Sosa play? True, there are a lot more teams now and it's a lot easier and quicker to get to the big leagues than it was forty or fifty years ago, but the best players in the game are as good or better than the best players of any era.

Another example of how you can't compare the players then and now: I was at a banquet for the Connecticut Sports Foundation in February 2004 and on the dais with me was Johnny Damon, the leadoff hitter for the Boston Red Sox. Now I'd watched Damon for five or six years and I always thought he was about five-foot-nine, 170 pounds, probably because he played the game like the prototypical leadoff hitter of my era. But as he was standing next to me, I realized he's six-foot-one, about 210 pounds, and then I grabbed his arm and it was like a tree trunk! All I could think of was Richie Ashburn, the definitive leadoff hitter in the 1950s and 1960s who is in the Hall of Fame with 2,574 hits and 234 stolen bases. Richie was five-foot-ten, 170 pounds, and hit 29 home runs his whole career. Damon, as of 2004, had 100 homers and already 214 stolen bases. Is Johnny Damon headed for the Hall of Fame? I can't say that. All I know is, when it's all over, his numbers are going to make Ashburn's pale in comparison. Yet Ashburn was every bit one of the best players of his time and belongs in the Hall of Fame—further demonstrating why you can't compare players from different eras.

What you *can* compare are teams. I'd have to say that because free agency, payroll concerns, and the related increase in player transition make it so hard to keep teams together today the teams of yesteryear were probably better. The Dodger team I played on in the 1950s had six future Hall of Famers—Jackie Robinson, Pee Wee Reese, Roy Campanella, Duke Snider, Sandy Koufax, and Don Drysdale—

and two others—Gil Hodges and Carl Furillo—for whom you could certainly make a Hall of Fame case. Not only that, they played together for a decade! Same with the Yankee teams of that era with Yogi Berra, Mickey Mantle, Whitey Ford, Phil Rizzuto, Gil McDougald, Hank Bauer, Joe Collins, Jerry Coleman, and Moose Skowron. That's why, when I think of how Joe Torre's Yankees were able to win four world championships in five years, in a three-tiered postseason system, I never cease to be amazed because we had so many key players, particularly pitchers, coming and going each year. I firmly believe the most significant factor in that team's success was that we were able to keep the core players—Jeter, Paul O'Neill, Tino Martinez, Bernie Williams, Andy Pettitte, Mariano Rivera, and the catchers, Joe Girardi and Jorge Posada—intact while other teams all seemed to be undergoing constant turnover with their key players. This all goes to that intangible in baseball they call chemistry.

Of course, if there's one thing that can upset the chemistry of the ballclub, it's money. When I played, the owners were able to control that aspect of the game. There was no free agency or salary arbitration and in order to curb the big bonuses being paid to the amateurs, baseball put in a rule that required any player signed for more than $4,000 to be kept on the major league roster. It turned out to be a very hurtful rule for the kids themselves because, for the most part, they hardly ever got to play and their skills wasted away for two years when they could have otherwise been refining them in the minors. My teammate, Sandy Koufax, who signed for $14,000 with the Dodgers in 1954, was one of the few who lived up to the greatness predicted for him, even though he appeared in only 28 games in his "bonus years" of 1955 and 1956 and didn't really get his career going into high gear until 1961.

But even the bonus rule didn't do much to keep clubs from handing out these huge sums of money to unproven amateur talent and so, in 1965, the owners came up with the amateur draft, which limited to one the number of teams a kid could sign with. Me? I got signed by the Dodgers for $2,500 in 1949 after my hometown team, the Cincinnati Reds, made a real bidding war out of it—with a counteroffer of $2,000. I'm proud to say I lived up to every penny of it.

Besides the baseball landscape, the size of players, their salaries, and their individual rights, the game itself—and how it was played,—was vastly different when I was a player. For instance: In 1954, my rookie season, Robin Roberts of the Phillies led the majors in innings pitched with 336⅔. If you're wondering—as I was—when the last time a pitcher hurled more than 300 innings in a season, it was Steve Carlton with 304 in 1980. Being that it's been more than twenty years now, I doubt we'll ever see the likes of a 300-inning pitcher again. Roberts also led the majors with 29 complete games in 1954 and, all told, there were 840 complete games pitched in the majors. By contrast, in 2003, the most innings pitched was 266 by Roy Halladay of the Toronto Blue Jays, while there were a grand total of 209 complete games. (I'll get into more detail later as to why, in my next baseball life, I definitely want to come back as a pitcher.)

Television was still pretty much in its early development in the 1950s so radio was the clubs' primary broadcasting outlet. Today, of course, it's the other way around with most clubs generating huge amounts of revenue by televising the bulk of their games on cable. This, in turn, has had more effect than anything else on the length of games. The clubs have got to provide the advertising time to pay their bills. The average time-of-game in 1955 was two hours and thirty-one minutes. In 2003, it was two hours and forty-eight minutes in the National League and even though baseball has taken steps to speed things up in recent years, they'll never get that quarter-hour back. While the increased between-innings advertising time is pretty much locked in, the one area where the commissioner's office could eliminate some wasted time is with the hitters getting in and out of the box. Unfortunately, only a few of the umpires are really vigilant about that, and all the other stuff—the music, the superstitious rituals—have gotten completely out of hand.

I'd have to say our guys with the Yankees were probably as bad as any in this regard when I was there. But the next time you're at a ballgame, just look around. While the pitcher is taking his warm-up throws, the hitter is talking to the fans in the box seats, even as the catcher throws the final warm-up pitch to second base. Now the batter knocks the weight off the end of his bat, lopes up to the plate, gets into the box, and starts digging his hole. Once he gets done with that, he backs off because he's got to fix his gloves. All this time, the pitcher is out there on the mound, waiting to pitch.

Meanwhile, they've all got their songs that are playing over the public-address system every time they come to bat. I've actually seen the game get held up because some guy's song hadn't started playing! I can just imagine how a Bob Gibson or an Early Wynn would have reacted if he had to wait for the batter's song to play before he could throw his first pitch! And most hitters step out of the box on every pitch. Barry Bonds is one exception. He never steps out of his hole and just waits to swing away, usually with the kind of results the pitcher would have preferred waiting for. Of course, you've got to remember. I was a guy who couldn't wait to get in there and hit. I was swinging the bat from the moment I left the on-deck circle.

But all the hitters' routines aside, I'd have to say the biggest reason games are longer now is because of how they're played. As I said earlier, the age of pitchers finishing what they started is long over. Each year, we see fewer and fewer complete games. As a result, this accounts for at least two to three more pitching changes per game by managers, and that doesn't include the extra visits to the mound to go over strategy or to gauge how the pitcher's feeling. Another factor is the increase in the running game from when I was playing. As a pitcher, you've got to stop the running game and that means stepping off the mound, throwing to first, pitching out, and so on, or else a team with good speed guys, like the Florida Marlins in 2003, will run you right out of the ballpark.

I'm not exactly sure when this pitching formula of a starter going six to seven innings, followed by a couple of set-up men, and finally the closer first started. I just know it's sure not Warren Spahn's or Robin Roberts' game any more. I love this "quality start" stat somebody came up with a few years ago. In today's game, a quality start is supposedly pitching six innings with giving up no more than three earned runs. How about that! Guy goes six innings, comes out of the game trailing 3–0 and as far as he's concerned, he's done his job. I somehow doubt if Gibson, Wynn, Drysdale, Roberts, Spahn, or Koufax would consider that a quality start.

I don't want this to sound like I'm complaining because I don't know whether any of this is right or wrong. All I'm saying is, this is how the game has changed.

What's interesting about this dramatic decrease in complete games and innings by pitchers is that it goes counter to everything the owners are trying to do today to keep payrolls down. In most cases, the best starting pitchers on a ballclub are also among the team's highest-paid players. That was the same forty to fifty years ago, only now they're being paid more to do less. I wonder if the owners have ever stopped to think how much the pitching costs them today just to win a ballgame. For instance, Roger Clemens, I'm told, was paid $10 million by the Yankees for 2003. He made 33 starts, which means he was paid something like $303,000 per start. I suppose in today's baseball economics that's not so bad, but unlike the pitchers of twenty years ago who completed the majority of their starts, Clemens completed one of his. Because of that, the Yankees needed at least two and sometimes three more pitchers to get the win. The set-up relievers are all making somewhere in the neighborhood of $2 million per year, and then you have Mariano Rivera, who's also paid about $10 million a year to close the games out. I'm no mathematics wizard—when I was in high school I bailed out of plane geometry to take wood shop—but think about what the owners pay per win today just to pitchers!

I'll say this, with the Yankees, Joe Torre got this formula down to a tee and, in 1996 we had the best set-up and closer relief team I've ever seen in Rivera, who would pitch the seventh and eighth innings (or just the eighth) and John Wetteland, who closed the game out in the ninth. We were able to make it a six-inning game where, if the opposing team was trailing at that point, they knew they had no chance. Not only did Rivera throw hard, he had a rubber arm, and when Wetteland left us to go to Texas and Rivera became our closer, Joe needed two men to replace him as the set-up guy.

And while we're talking about Rivera here, I've got to say this guy was nothing short of super human. I don't know if Yankee fans realize how important he was to all those championships we won in my eight years there. Without him, I don't know if we win even one of 'em. Just look at these stats: In 96 innings of postseason work from

1995 to 2003, Rivera gave up just 60 hits and 12 walks while striking out 77! His overall earned run average for that period was 0.75; his batting average against, .176. He was successful in 30 of 32 save opportunities. I can't imagine if we'll ever see a more dominating post-season relief pitcher for that length of time. And even though Rivera hasn't yet reached the ten-year eligibility standard, I would have to say he doesn't have to do anything more to be a first-ballot Hall of Famer.

Here's something else people might not know about Rivera. He's one hell of a center fielder. That's right. The man can play center field as good as anyone I've ever seen. I base this on watching him shag flies during pregame batting practice for eight years. He's a natural out there, all over the place, covering ground from right-center to left-center like Willie Mays. I just loved the guy and I know of no better person in baseball.

One of my everlasting memories of Rivera will be the three-inning, 48-pitch effort he gave us in Game Seven of the 2003 ALCS against Boston that enabled us to finally win the game on Aaron Boone's home run. Looking back, I have to laugh at some of the second-guessing Joe got for using Rivera for two innings at a time in the postseason. You're just not supposed to do that with your closer, or so the common thinking goes. But when you get into the post-season when everything is now do or die, the formula you may have used over the 162-game regular season no longer applies—especially when it comes to using the greatest closer in the history of the game. Believe me, when Mo was going back out there for that third inning against the Red Sox, nobody was counting his pitches—and it turned out to be the only inning in which he retired the side in order, two of them by strikeouts.

And this brings up another one of the facts of life in today's baseball that *is* a pet peeve of mine—pitch counts.

It's a hell of a thing when you're a pitcher and the pitching coach says, "I hope we can get six to seven innings out of this guy." What's wrong with nine? The problem is, we're all hung up with stats today. A pitcher's not satisfied with using five pitches to get himself out of an inning. He wants to strike out all three batters. Mike Mussina is an example of what I mean. Mike's a terrific pitcher, don't get me wrong. But he'll get strike one, strike two on a batter and then, the next thing you know, the count goes full because he's nibbling away trying to get that strikeout instead of just getting the guy to hit a ground ball to the shortstop. By the sixth inning he's already thrown over 100 pitches. Jeff Nelson is another example. He'll go strike one, strike two, and you can bet the ranch he'll go 3-2 with three of those sweeping curves of his because he wants the strikeouts so he can go to his agent after the season and show he's got all these strikeouts per inning.

One of the primary reasons Robin Roberts was able to log all those innings was because he threw strikes. He led the National League in wins four times, in complete games five times, in strikeouts twice, and won 286 games. He also gave up more home runs— 505—than any pitcher in the history of baseball, but I'll bet the vast majority of them were solo shots. When Robbie got a hitter 0-2, he didn't nibble. He came right at you. When he was in a jam, there were no trick pitches. You knew what you were gonna get—gas— and you'd better be ready for it.

I know this sounds "old school" and I suppose it is, but I believe pitchers now are babied like never before, to the point where we've become obsessed with pitch counts. It starts from the moment they sign their first contract and report to the minor leagues. Immediately, they're on a pitch count and it never stops. We program pitchers today *not* to think about pitching nine innings. That's just the way it is. Take a look sometime at all the minor league statistics after any season now. I guarantee you won't see more than a handful of pitchers with 150 or more innings.

My first experience with pitch counts was when I was managing the Knoxville club in the Southern League in 1967. We were playing Birmingham, a Kansas City A's farm team managed by John McNamara, who later went on to a long and successful managing career in the majors. McNamara's pitcher that day was a Cuban right-handed curveballer named George Lauzerique, who was nineteen years old at the time. Well, the game is going along and we're into the seventh inning and Lauzerique is pitching a no-hitter. All of a sudden, I look up and Johnny Mac is walking to the mound to take him out! It turned out Lauzerique had reached his quota of 100 pitches, set down by the A's front office, and Johnny Mac had no choice but to follow orders. They put pitch counts on these pitchers to supposedly save their arms. It didn't help Lauzerique, though. He got into a total of 34 games in the majors over four seasons before hurting his shoulder, and was out of baseball by the time he was twenty-three.

Today, every pitching coach in baseball keeps a pitch counter on him in the dugout. What I'd like to know is, who's smart enough to know how many pitches or innings to put on a pitcher? I was always amused when a pitcher would come into the dugout after five strong innings and the pitching coach would go up to him and ask: "How do you feel?" What's wrong with letting them come to *you*? Instead, we *encourage* them to come out of games. How would you like me to be the manager and go down the dugout after five innings and ask Drysdale how he feels? I'd be lucky he didn't throw the ball at me and snarl: "How did *that* feel?" When I managed, we had pitch counts, but I never paid any attention to them. I always managed with my gut feelings. I always felt that what I *saw* with my own eyes was far more telling about a pitcher than what some pitch counter said.

One of those times was in the fifth and deciding game of the 1989 NLCS in which I was managing the Cubs against the San Francisco Giants. My starter, Mike Bielecki, had pitched brilliantly through the first six innings, limiting the Giants to two harmless singles. But in the seventh, Will Clark, who absolutely killed us in that series, hit a triple and was brought home on a sacrifice fly by Kevin Mitchell to tie the score at 1–1. I could have taken Bielecki out after Clark's triple, but my gut told me he still had enough left in the tank, and I chalked off that hit to a guy who was simply on fire. The next inning, though, Bielecki walked three straight batters and after I brought in my closer, Mitch Williams, Clark wound up beating us with a 2-run single. I went out to talk to Bielecki after the second walk that inning and he assured me he felt as strong as he had in the first inning. If Bielecki had expressed any reservations whatsoever, I'd have taken him out right there, but he said it with such conviction my gut told me to leave him in and give him the chance to pitch out of this. In that particular situation, my trust in my gut was misguided. I guess I should have asked my pitching coach, Dick Pole, what the pitch count clicker said.

I once took Williams out of a game, in the midst of a save situation, but it didn't have anything to do with pitch counts. We were playing the Phillies in Wrigley Field late in the 1989 season. Mitch had 36 saves for me that year, but this wasn't going to be one of them. It's a 1-run game and Mitch comes in and gets the first two batters out in the ninth. Now, up comes Mike Schmidt, who's got more home runs than any other right-handed hitter in Wrigley Field, and in the bullpen, I've got a right-hander named Les Lancaster who's been hotter than a firecracker for me. I had never taken Mitch out in a save situation up to then and as I walked out to the mound, I knew he couldn't figure out what I was up to.

I walked up to him, put out my hand and said: "My man, you did a great job, but I'm making a change." He looked at me in disbelief and then hollered, "You're not taking me out!" and we got into a beef right there on the mound. He finally ran into the dugout, grabbed his jacket, and went up into the clubhouse.

In my first meeting with Mitch that spring after we'd gotten him from the Texas Rangers, he told me that Bobby Valentine, his manager in Texas, hated him and had accused him of being a selfish player. He assured me that wasn't the case; that he was a team player and he'd gotten a bum rap from Valentine. I said to him: "You're pitching for the Cubs now, so I don't want to hear any more of this."

Well, after the game—which Lancaster sealed for us by getting Schmidt out—I told Yosh Kawano, our clubhouse man, to send Mitch up to my office. Mitch walked in and he was still hot.

"I'm your closer," he said. "How could you take me out?"

"Did we win?" I shot back.

"Yeah," he said.

"Then I don't ever want to hear about that stuff about Bobby Valentine calling you selfish."

He was embarrassed and we never had another problem, other than the fact that he'd drive me crazy with that high-wire act of his every time I brought him in to close a game out for us. After every save the rest of that year, he'd go past my office on the way out the back door of the clubhouse and kid me.

"Well, did you lose any more hair?" he'd say.

"Just a few," I'd answer.

Look at me today. I owe most of this bald head of mine to Mitch Williams.

My favorite story about pitch counts involves my old pal Johnny Podres, who was pitching coach for the Phillies in the mid-1990s when Jim Fregosi was the manager. Pods of course was old school like me when it came to pitch counts. He paid no attention to them, but, rather, just watched his pitcher. If in his opinion his pitcher was throwing horse shit, despite having thrown only 80 pitches or so, and Fregosi would ask: "How many pitches he got?" Pods would answer: "A hundred eleven and he's spent!" Then on other occasions when his pitcher might have thrown 119 pitches but in Pods's opinion was still pitching well, he'd answer Fregosi by saying: "He's only at 86, Skip."

One more little aside here about pitch counts: On July 2, 1963, Juan Marichal and Warren Spahn hooked up in one of the greatest pitching duels of all time, matching shutouts for fifteen innings before Willie Mays won it for the Giants with a home run in the sixteenth. In the game, Spahn—who, by the way, was forty-two—threw 201 pitches, while Marichal threw 227. If that ever happened today, both managers would have been fired. But it's sad to think a great pitching duel like that will never be allowed again. Incidentally, Spahn went on to win 23 games and lead the league in complete games with 22 that year. Marichal likewise showed no ill effects of his labor from that game, winning 20 or more games in five of the next six seasons. What can I say? It was a very different game then.

Another factor in the decrease in innings pitched is, without question, the evolution of the five-man rotation. I'm not sure when this started becoming the norm in baseball, but my pal Jim Kaat, who's a student of pitching, seems to think it started with my old Dodger teammate, Rube Walker, when he was pitching coach of the New York Mets under Gil Hodges and Yogi Berra in the late 1960s and early 1970s. I never talked to Rube about it, although I do know those Mets staffs had five pretty good young starting pitchers in Tom Seaver, Jerry Koosman, Nolan Ryan, Gary Gentry, and Jim McAndrew, and they also had veteran guys like Don Cardwell and Ray Sadecki who they worked into their rotation. They all spread out their innings so I guess maybe it did start there.

I'll be honest here. I was proud of Jack McKeon, one of my fellow old-school geezers, when he thumbed his nose at all the critics who said he was crazy for pitching Josh Beckett on three days' rest in the sixth game of the 2003 World Series. McKeon's attitude was that Beckett was young and strong and that pitching on one less day of rest shouldn't be a problem. Besides, he said, Beckett was his best pitcher and the point was not to let the Series *get* to a seventh game. I wish he had held him back another day after the way Beckett made fools of McKeon's critics by pitching a complete game, 5-hit shutout over the Yankees. I could only sit back and marvel at how easy he made it look. That and think to myself, "Three days rest, my ass!"

It just seems to me that once starting pitchers began pitching on four days' rest instead of three, the owners, whether they realized it or not, started getting less for their money. Meanwhile, as they were adding starters to the rotation, baseball began expanding from sixteen teams to the thirty there are today. The result today is fourteen more teams, at the same time you have extra starters in the rotation, specialized set-up men in the bullpen, and closers who the manager is required to pitch in every game where there's a save situation. Again, I'm not saying there's anything wrong with this. I'm just saying this is how much the game has changed. I can remember when I was a player and, with guys completing games so often, there'd be a number of times during the season when we'd be carrying only eight pitchers. No question, expansion has spread the talent thin in baseball, especially the pitchers. But even as the owners were beginning to expand, they had begun the process of paying two to three extra guys to do a job one man had pretty much been doing for eighty years.

If you sat around having beers with Roberts, Johnny Podres, Lew Burdette, or any of the workhorse pitchers I've been referring to from my playing days, and you brought up the way pitchers are handled today, they wouldn't know what you're talking about. They'd all tell you that the biggest problem with pitchers today is that they don't throw enough. Kaat—who, by the way, won 283 games in the big leagues—says the same thing and points to Johnny Sain, another old-timer from my era, as the guy who had the most influence on him as a pitcher. Sain was Kaat's pitching coach with the Minnesota Twins in 1965 and 1966 and was a strong proponent of pitchers throwing more than once between starts.

"Johnny believed in exercising your arm every day," Kaat told me. "He felt it made you stronger and the muscles less susceptible to injury."

Kaat said it's no surprise that the one pitching coach today who has his pitchers throw twice between starts is Leo Mazzone of the Atlanta Braves, who was a disciple of Sain's. It's pretty hard to ignore the recent success of the Braves' pitchers, or the fact that, their two best, Greg Maddux and Tom Glavine, never got hurt.

Supposedly, the five-man rotation was designed to save pitchers' arms. So how then do you explain that one-third of them break down anyway? That's not from me. I'm not a pitcher. This is from guys like Kaat and Roberts and Spahn who pitched 280 innings per year.

And speaking of pitchers getting hurt, this is probably the one area where the game has really advanced to the point where it sometimes seems absurd. Years ago, long before they had the medical advances they have today with the ability to perform arthroscopic surgery or a "Tommy John" tendon transplant operation, a pitcher's arm started hurting and they simply called it a "dead arm." Tommy Lasorda loves telling the joke about how, in his playing days, the team trainer carried around a bottle of rubbing alcohol for when the pitchers would complain of sore arms, only he usually drank it all himself. That's really not so far off. We never heard of a rotator cuff, and we'll never know how many pitchers back then tore theirs and simply pitched through it until they couldn't take the pain any longer. I don't know how many pitchers I played with whose careers ended because, as they put it, their arm finally went "dead."

Nowadays, of course, the slightest twinge in the shoulder or elbow and the pitcher gets shut down. They send 'em out for X rays and dye tests and even when all of those come up negative they usually prescribe for the pitcher to miss a start. I understand the caution. You're dealing with millions and millions of dollars worth of pitching arms here. But I have to say the extremes they take today in caution make me shake my head.

This is what I mean. A guy is coming off an arm injury and the club announces he's starting his rehab. "He did 'long toss' for six minutes today," the media relations department announces. Then, a couple of days later, it's announced, "He threw on flat ground today and might be ready to throw off the mound in a couple of days." Finally, the sign that the guy is really making progress (in other words he's probably another three weeks away from actually pitching in a real game) is when they tell us, "He threw thirty-five pitches in the bullpen." Can you tell me what the hell all this means? I have to giggle because I can't relate to any of it.

I'll give you another "rehab" dandy that involved a hitter. One year when I was with the Yankees, one of our outfielders was on rehab for some sort of injury down in Tampa when the word came back that he'd completed a successful session in which he'd taken 30 swings—underwater! I have to admit this one really left me dumbfounded. My only question was: Saltwater or fresh?

I seem to remember Gregg Jefferies, who played for the Mets, Phillies, and Cardinals in the '80s and '90s, was one guy who had a made a big deal of developing his swing by hitting underwater. He was a steady .300 hitter his first few years in the majors, so maybe there was some merit to it after all. His career, however, was curtailed by injuries and I wonder if maybe he just got waterlogged.

One change in the game I'm not crazy about but I *can* relate to just the same is the relaxation of the no-fraternization rule. Years ago, baseball prohibited any public fraternization before games because, it was felt, it gave the fans the wrong impression about whether these teams were really intent on beating each other. But when you go to a game today and get there early, you'll see the home team loosening up in right field and half of them are shaking hands and wrapping their arms around the guys from the visiting team. Once free agency came into being in baseball and they did away with the restriction of trading players from league to league, players began moving around far more frequently. It's rare today for any player to remain on the same team for more than five or six years and as a result, you've got a whole lot of reunions going on during the course of the season. That's just the way it is, but what seems to have been forgotten is that *this is your opponent.* I don't know, maybe the fans don't care, but I still wonder if they see this and don't ask themselves: "Do these guys really want to beat each other?"

A lot of times, they might be asking that same question during the course of the game when, with one out and a ground ball to short, the runner on first takes a routine slide into second base, allowing the defensive team to make a relatively easy double play. I was taught to always slide hard and try to break up the double play. Too often today, though, you do that and it's as if the second baseman or shortstop thinks you stole his candy.

I know some players today will be rubbed wrong by my statements, but it's a fact. I'm not saying they don't think they're playing hard. I just think they ought to see pictures or films of guys like Hal McRae, Frank Robinson, Darryl Spencer, or Bob Cerv (to name four I'd put on my all-come-to-beat-you team) sliding into second base. When I was playing short or second, I was always aware of the base runner at first, and more often than not it was somebody I knew I was going to have to get out of the way of in a hurry if I had to cover the bag. I'm just not too sure there's too many base runners today who command the same respect—and fear—from the fielders.

Of those four hard-nosed guys I mentioned, both McRae and Robinson went on to become managers, and I often thought about asking them for their private thoughts about the entourages of "care-takers" afforded today's players. On any given day in the Yankee clubhouse during my eight years there you'd see personal trainers, a team psychiatrist, and even a masseuse! These people all travled with the club, too.

I watched with amusement in the spring of 2003 when the commissioner, Bud Selig, announced a crackdown on all unauthorized people in the clubhouse. I understand it was a response to the commissioner's concerns about steroids, but I wonder if the commissioner remembered what it used to be like forty years ago when I was playing. For one thing, the clubhouses back then were barely big enough to accommodate the twenty-five players, manager, and coaches. In Ebbets Field we had a tiny trainer's room with one rubbing table in it. It wasn't necessary to have more than one table because we had just one trainer and if a guy needed a back rub, the trainer did it.

Today, teams have their own masseuse, and I've got to tell you, I've seen guys getting a rub from the masseuse every day who don't get into a game for a week at a time!

Obviously, we never had any weight rooms either. Nobody lifted weights when I played. Nowadays weight programs are organized and most clubs have their own manuals, which they give to the players. I personally never believed in weight lifting but, as a manager, my attitude was if the player felt it was necessary for him, fine, as long as the club was supervising it. I didn't have to deal with the personal trainer issue that has come about in recent years. Most players today seem to have their own personal trainers, which is fine, but it became a problem when they'd have trainers with them all the time, including in the clubhouse. At least, by his mandate, Selig may have taken the clubs off the hook in regard to policing the clubhouses.

I'm not sure when teams began employing their own in-house psychiatrists, although I suspect it had something to do with the drug stuff that happened in the '70s. I'm sure these guys serve a very useful purpose—it's just that I never imagined anything like shrinks in baseball. Maybe I should have because there are a lot of people who probably think I've acted a little nuts at times and needed one.

I mentioned earlier about the fans' perception of how hard the game is being played. I might also add that the fans themselves have changed. When I first came up to the big leagues with the Dodgers, the fans at Ebbets Field were almost like an extension of our families. There was most definitely an intimacy with the fans, which, I'm sure, had a lot to do with the small ballpark. At the same time, when we were asked for our autograph, we knew it was because the fan looked at it as having a part of us. Nowadays, autographs have become big business and you can never know whether a fan wants an autograph for a keepsake or to sell it. You certainly know what the deal is when you go on a road trip and arrive at your hotel at four o'clock in the morning and there's a group of eight or ten guys waiting there with stacks of cards and photos. For the most part, the players will just ignore them. You hate to deprive a kid of your autograph, but a lot of times the grown-ups will send their kids to get the autographs, which they then intend to sell. As a result, you don't know where to draw the line.

As for the overall demeanor of the fans, I think they may be a little harder on the players today just because of the money. Remember, when I was playing, a lot of us weren't making as much as a lot of the fans, and most of the players had to get second jobs in the off-season to make ends meet. I'm sure there's a lot of resentment today of players making $5 million to $10 million a year.

Now if this all sounds as if I'm saying it's a kinder, gentler game being played by bigger and wealthier players, well, I guess I am. At the same time, I've got to say it's still a great game. Nothing that's been done to it has dimmed my enthusiasm in the least for coming to the ballpark every day. The publisher of this book tells me that all these opinions and observations are part of the "zen" that's in the title. To be perfectly honest, I have no idea what that word means. A more appropriate title, in my opinion, might have been: "Rantings of a Baseball Humpty."

# CHAPTER
# 6

# Brooklyn, 1955

I've said it a thousand times: Nobody's been luckier than me to have had the baseball life I've had. I mean, think of it, for fifty-six years I've always had a baseball uniform and never had to look anywhere else for a job. (I can't imagine where I'd have ever looked anyway since I don't know anything else!) I've had the privilege of playing for some of the best managers the game has ever known, people like Charlie Dressen, Fred Hutchinson, Herman Franks, Gil Hodges, and even Casey Stengel. I've also had the privilege of calling some of the greatest players of all time—Jackie Robinson, Pee Wee Reese, Sandy Koufax, Don Drysdale, Duke Snider, Roy Campanella, Gil Hodges, Ernie Banks, Billy Williams, Lou Brock, Richie Ashburn, Frank Robinson—my teammates. I've got six World Series championship rings and been to nearly a dozen All-Star Games—believe it or not, even one of them as a player! And I've worked in the best baseball towns in the country—New York, Boston, Chicago—as well as my two hometowns, Cincinnati and now Tampa Bay. Could anyone ask for more?

Of course, you look at a travelogue resume like this and your first thought must be: This guy could never seem to hold a job, going from one organization to another as he did. I have known what it is to get released, sold, and fired. Fortunately, there's always seemed to be somebody on the other end who's wanted me. But of all the places I've been and all the experiences I've had, I know that, in my heart of hearts, I'll always be a Dodger, and there will never be a season quite so special for me as a player than 1955.

I say this mainly because the Dodgers were the team I grew up with, having signed with them out of high school in 1949, and you could certainly make a case for those Brooklyn Dodger teams of the 1950s being among the greatest ever assembled. In Jackie, Pee Wee, Campy, Duke, Sandy, and Drysdale you've got six Hall of Famers right there, and I still believe Gil will eventually get there too. Still, for all that talent, they were only able to win one World Series for Brooklyn and that was 1955. It's hard to believe it was nearly a half-century ago, but like everyone else associated with it who's still around, I never get tired of reliving it.

I was technically a rookie in 1955—having had a brief, 24-game "cup of coffee" major league debut in 1954—so I wasn't really in tune with the "wait 'til next year" mindset of baseball fans in Brooklyn back then. This was the result of the Dodgers having lost to the Yankees in the 1947, 1949, 1952, and 1953 World Series. All I knew was we had one hell of a collection of baseball talent and I couldn't believe I was going to be part of it. After managing to overcome my first serious beaning, at Triple-A St. Paul in 1953 by hitting .291 with 17 homers in 97 games there the next year, I felt I'd proven to the Dodger brass I didn't need to spend any more time in the minor leagues. Nevertheless, when I made the team out of spring training in 1955, I knew it was going to be strictly as a backup to Pee Wee at short, which meant getting myself prepared to spend a lot of idle time on the "pine." But then, as so often has happened in my career, fate stepped in and made me the accidental opening-day shortstop for the Dodgers when Pee Wee's back went out on him.

Even though I had played some in 1954, I had some opening-day jitters. Any ballplayer who says he doesn't is lying. This is part of being an athlete. And in my case, it was especially a nervous time because when you're a humpty suddenly playing for a real good team, you don't want to screw up for fear you could cost this team a pennant.

As it was, the Dodgers won the 1955 National League pennant in a runaway, 13½ games over the Milwaukee Braves, and thanks to a record-setting 10-0 start to the season, were in first place all the way. I am proud to say I was the Dodger shortstop through that entire season-opening winning streak—Pee Wee was ready to come back after it had reached 8, but our manager, Walt Alston, didn't want to break up a winning combination, so he left me out there until we finally lost. I used to kid Pee Wee that, were it not for him hurting his back, the Dodgers might not have won in 1955 either! But for the first three months of the season, most of it *with* Pee Wee at short, we were about the hottest team in baseball history. After the 10-0 start, we won 22 of our first 24 and were 55-22 on July 4, 12½ games in first place.

Even though I resumed my proper place on the bench with the rest of the humpties that season, I did have my moments. In the record-setting tenth-straight win to open the season, I went 4-for-4 with a homer and 3 RBIs in a 14–4 rout of the Phillies, and on September 9 against the Cubs, long after the race was decided, I had one of my greatest games in baseball with 2 homers, one a grand slam off a right-hander named Bill Tremel, and 6 RBIs.

I was reminded of our 10-game winning streak to open the season when the Yankees got off to their torrid 21–6 April start in 2003 in which our five starters—Roger Clemens, Andy Pettitte, Mike Mussina, David Wells, and Jeff Weaver—were a combined 16-0 up until April 24. During the course of the 1955 Dodgers' 10-0 start, six different starters—Don Newcombe, Carl Erskine, Billy Loes, Johnny Podres, Russ Meyer, and Joe Black—got wins, and, don't forget, this was well before the five-man rotation. It seemed Alston had a wealth of starting pitching to start the season, but as is so often the case with pitchers, they all either went into slumps or broke down. Before the season was over, we would need an infusion of youth from Koufax and two late-season emergency starters from Triple-A, Roger Craig and Don Bessent.

Koufax was a nineteen-year old "bonus baby" that year and hadn't pitched in too many games when Alston finally tapped him in late August to start against the Cincinnati Reds. It was his first major league start and he threw a 2-hit shutout, striking out 14, most by any pitcher in the league that year. A week later, he shut out Pittsburgh, but shortly after that, Alston stopped using him and went back to his veterans. It seemed the Dodgers were afraid of Sandy's wildness early on in his career. They just didn't trust him and because of that, one of the greatest pitching careers of all time had a late start, not to mention an all-too-early finish. I know because, as one of the humpties who had to hit against Sandy most of that year when he was getting his innings in pitching batting practice, I screamed the loudest about his control. That was my self-defense for the fact that I couldn't hit this teenage kid with a snow shovel.

Newcombe was, without question, our warhorse pitcher that year. He finished the season at 20-5 with 17 complete games, 143 strikeouts, and just 38 walks in 233 innings. At one point, he won 10 straight decisions and was 14-1 at the All-Star break. But even he had some problems. He won only 1 game after August 1, and did not really get his hot streak going until an incident in early May when Alston suspended him and fined him $300 for refusing to pitch batting practice. Newk was really hot about that and went to Buzzie Bavasi, the general manager, asking to be traded. Buzzie, typically, told him what he could do with his threat and backed Alston to the hilt.

"Get it through your skull," he hollered at Newk. "You're not going anywhere and you're not managing this club."

Newk, realizing he'd made a huge mistake, apologized to Buzzie and then took his remaining anger out on the Cubs, shutting them out on 1 hit while facing the minimum 27 batters in the process.

One of the main reasons Newcombe completed so many games for the Dodgers was because Alston never had a need to pinch-hit for him. He was one of the best hitters on the club. He hit .359 in 1955 and set a National League record for home runs by a pitcher with 7. He was also Alston's best pinch hitter, going 8-for-21. Not only that, Newcombe could run the bases as good as anyone. He was just a tremendous athlete. In a game against the Pirates in late May, he drove in a couple of runs and stole home! When was the last time you saw a pitcher do that? People may have forgotten too that after Newk's pitching career in the majors ended in 1960 he signed on in Japan—as an outfielder.

I've always been saddened by the fact that the designated hitter rule has turned good-hitting pitchers into a dying breed. When I played in American Legion ball, the best player on the team was usually the pitcher. Jim Brosnan, who pitched for the Chicago Cubs and Cincinnati Reds and then went on to become a best-selling author, was on my first American Legion team, and he was a very good-hitting pitcher. Warren Spahn was a great hitter and that was why he, too, completed so many games. Back then, pitchers took pride in their hitting, but now with the DH rule in the American League, half of them never even take a swing in the batting cage during the regular season. I know when I was with the Yankees and we'd get to the World Series, there was so little time for the pitchers to work on their hitting that all we concerned ourselves with was making sure they could at least bunt.

Over the years, people have always debated what it was that made the Yankees so superior to the Dodgers in all those World Series. From what I know, it was pitching. We always had a lot of really good pitchers, but for some reason, they never put it all together in the same season and same World Series as the Yankees' bunch—Allie Reynolds, Vic Raschi, Eddie Lopat and Whitey Ford—seemed to do. In 1955, however, even though our guys all had their slumps and injuries, we had more good pitching than in any other season I was there. Everybody on the staff made a vital contribution.

After Newcombe, Erskine won 11 games before being hampered by shoulder and elbow problems the last two months. My buddy, Johnny Podres, who I'll get to later, won 9 games. Billy Loes was on the disabled list twice with arm trouble but was still 10–4. And Clem Labine, who I've always felt was the most underrated Dodger pitcher of that whole era, had perhaps the best season of any of them, leading the National League with 60 appearances, including 8 spot starts, while finishing up at 13-5 with 11 saves. I've mentioned earlier what Koufax contributed, and then on July 17, with only Newcombe seemingly not hurting for us, Alston reached down to our two Triple-A clubs, Montreal and St. Paul, and brought up a pair of twenty-four-year-old right-handers, Bessent and Craig, to pitch a doubleheader versus the Reds. Even though we still had a comfortable lead, it was a huge gamble on Alston's part, sending not one but *two* pitchers out there for their major league debuts on the same day. If both of them had flopped, it could have been a huge blow to our morale.

Well, Craig, who only the year before was pitching in Class-B ball, pitched a 3-hitter to win the opener 6–2, and Bessent pitched almost as well in winning the nightcap, 8–5, in which he tired in the ninth and was knocked out on a 3-run rally. Bessent went on to win 8 straight, and the two of them combined to go 13-4 the rest of the year. We called them "Vitamins B and C" and I became pals with both of them in all the years later. Along with Don Hoak and Ed Roebuck, another relief pitcher who had a great first half in 1955, we were the "young turks" on that team—the guys who all came up from the farm system that year and didn't know any better as far as all the previous disappointments in the World Series. I liked to call us "the humpty squad" because we were definitely the support group for Jackie, Pee Wee, Newk, Erskine, Labine, Duke, and the rest of those veteran guys.

Many years later, I wound up coaching third base for Craig when he was managing the Giants in 1987, and we still keep in touch. Roebuck and I have been close friends since 1951 when we were minor league teammates in Elmira, New York, and got married on the same day there. After we both got traded by the Dodgers, we ended up teammates again with the Washington Senators in the early 1960s. Sadly, Hoak and Bessent are both gone, much too early. Hoak was a real scrapper, an ex-marine who was always getting in fights—invariably winding up on his back. Hodges, who was also an ex-marine, used to kid him all the time, calling him "canvas back."

The Bessent-Craig doubleheader success on July 17 kind of stabilized us after injuries had begun to take a toll on the great start we'd had. We didn't do much sweating after that and wound up clinching the pennant on September 7, the earliest clinching in National League history to that point. Our final margin of victory—13½ games over the second-place Braves—was the biggest in the NL since 1944.

Despite the relative ease with which we won in 1955, the year was not without some internal unrest. Besides Newcombe's flare-up with Alston in May, Jackie's feud with Alston was always simmering in the background. In addition to that, Russ the "Mad Monk" Meyer, another one of our veteran starting pitchers, complained about not being used enough. Then, late in the season, Duke got into it with the fans over getting booed when he was in the midst of a bad slump.

Jackie and Alston never really got along, I think probably because Jackie, who was nearing the end of his career when Alston took over in 1954, resented being rested frequently. It's always hard for the manager when a proud, veteran Hall of Fame–caliber player gets to the point where his skills have deteriorated and he's not ready to concede that fact.

One prime example I can think of was when Tony LaRussa took over as manager of the St. Louis Cardinals at around the time Ozzie Smith had lost a step at shortstop. Ozzie hit .199 in 1995 and that winter the Cardinals acquired Royce Clayton from the Giants to take over at short. Only Ozzie wasn't ready to give way. And, so, when LaRussa set up a platoon system in 1996 with the idea of getting the most out of both shortstops, Ozzie fumed. Just the same, he managed to hit a very respectable .282 in that, his last year, and five years later, was elected to the Hall of Fame on his first shot. But unfortunately he never could bring himself to mend fences with LaRussa.

The same thing happened with me when I was managing the Cubs in 1988 and Goose Gossage came over to us from the San Diego Padres—although, in our case, it eventually had a happy ending. I had remembered Goose from 1983 when I was a coach for the Yankees and he was in the prime of his career as the most intimidating relief pitcher in baseball. But he was thirty-six when he came to the Cubs and he'd lost something off his fastball and slider. As a result, he was getting beaten up a lot as my closer and when I finally had to start looking to alternatives, Goose lashed out at me and accused me of losing confidence in him.

Like I said, these guys all have their pride and it's tough to accept that you can't do it any more like you used to. Inevitably, they want to shoot the messenger, which is usually the manager. Goose and I went a few years without talking to each other and then one day we ran into each other in spring training and I decided to go up to him and clear the air. Well, it seemed he wanted to do the same thing and, from that day on, we've been the best of friends. I absolutely love the guy, to the point that when I was coaching for the Yankees and they gave me a new uniform each year to coincide with my number of years in baseball, I told them I didn't want 54 because that was Goose's and, in my opinion, it ought to be retired.

But getting back to Jackie and Alston, I don't think their differences ever really got settled either. In 1955, Jackie was thirty-six years old but coming off an All-Star season in which he'd hit .311. There was no question, though, he'd lost a step in the field, and during the late spring training exhibition games Alston was resting him a lot—I'm sure with the idea of preserving him for the regular season. Jackie, however, didn't see it that way and gave it to Alston in the papers.

"If Alston doesn't want to play me," he said, "then let him get rid of me. When I'm fit, I've got as much right to be playing as any man on this team. He knows it—or maybe he doesn't."

A few days later when Alston was asked about his opening-day lineup, he shot back: "I don't see why I should tell the damned press anything. As for Robinson, if he has any complaints, why the hell don't he come to me instead of the writers?"

Meanwhile, a week after that, even Campy, the most mild-mannered guy on the team, got into it with Alston after starting off the season hitting eighth in the batting order. "That's fine encouragement, he's giving me," he said, "having me hit with the batboy."

We humpties didn't pay much attention to all of this. We were just glad to be in the majors and every so often getting the opportunity to play when Alston was resting his proud veterans. It was, I'm sure, an uneasy situation for Alston as a second-year manager and career minor leaguer trying to handle this team of veteran superstars. In the end, though, everybody seemed to get past whatever gripes they had with the manager and, as the season wore on, found themselves constantly picking each other up while taking it out on the opposition.

For most of the year Jackie was bothered by assorted injuries, especially to his knee, and he fell off to .256 and got into only 105 games. But he had his moments. In late April, the day after the Giants snapped our opening 10-game winning streak, we were playing them again and Jackie got brushed back by Sal Maglie. Now you have to understand, the Dodgers hated Maglie because we felt he was a headhunter, most often against *our guys*. He didn't get his nickname "The Barber" for nothing. So after getting brushed back, Jackie bunted the next pitch to the first base side of the infield in hopes of getting a piece of Maglie. But Maglie never budged from the mound and, instead, it was Davey Williams, the Giants' second baseman, covering first, who got the full force of Jackie's fury. Jackie knocked him ass over tea kettle and Williams wound up in the Mayo Clinic with a back injury.

Late in the season, Jackie stole home for the eighteenth time in his career in a game against the Cardinals—and that brings to mind another lost art in baseball. I don't think there's a more exciting play than someone stealing home, but you just don't see it anymore, primarily because pitchers don't wind up with men on bases anymore. Heck, most of 'em pitch out of the stretch with nobody on now. About the only time you'll see a steal of home today is when it's part of a double steal.

Meanwhile, as for Campy, he quickly convinced Alston he was no number-eight hitter. Part of the reason, I think, Alston started Campy off there was because he wasn't sure about his physical condition. In 1954, Campy had been bothered by a bad bone spur in his hand all season long and he hit a career-low .207 after winning MVP honors the year before. He had surgery to correct the problem over the winter and got into a hot streak right off the bat. By late April, he was back in the cleanup spot and remained there for the rest of the year. He hit .318 with 32 homers and 107 RBI and was voted National League MVP for the third time.

In my opinion, you could have made an MVP case for Duke as well. During those torrid first few months of the season when we were running away from the pack, Duke carried us. At one point in July, he was ahead of Babe Ruth's record home run pace—he wound up with 42—and after his first 77 games, he had 84 RBIs! He was also one of the best defensive center fielders ever, although he never got his due credit there because of Willie Mays playing for the Giants at the same time. But where Willie had the advantage of all that room to chase down fly balls at the Polo Grounds, Duke was confined in Ebbets Field and didn't have the chance to show off his range.

I don't know of any center fielder who could jump higher than Duke—Branch Rickey, who signed him for the Dodgers, used to say he had springs in his legs—and in 1954 he made a catch in Shibe Park in Philadelphia that no one who saw it will ever forget. The Phillies' "Puddin' Head" Jones hit a ball to center that looked like it was going out when Duke climbed right up the wall with his spikes, reached up, and snared it.

Sometime in mid-July of 1955, Duke got hit with a flu virus that left him really weakened. After a day on the bench, he came back and helped us beat the Reds with 2 homers, but after that, the flu thing seemed to halt his momentum. He was in a slump for most of

August and eventually the fans started getting on him. Finally, between the slump and the booing, Duke had had enough and just blew up. He gathered the writers in the clubhouse and ripped into the fans.

"The Brooklyn fans are the worst in the league," he said. "They're a lousy bunch of frontrunners and they don't deserve a pennant."

Well, you can just imagine how that went over with Buzzie, but it was the captain who took it upon himself to scold Duke.

"You gotta knock that stuff off, Duke," Pee Wee told him. "It does nobody any good, especially you, to get on the fans."

"Ah," Duke retorted, "I can win 'em back with one swing of the bat!"

Sure enough, the next night, Duke went 3-for-3, with a homer, a triple, and 3 RBIs to snap his slump in a 10–4 win over the Cardinals, and the Ebbets crowd cheered him like never before.

Pee Wee, of course, came to be about my closest friend in baseball and I miss him dearly. One of the real highlights for me that 1955 season was July 22 when the Dodgers gave him a night in honor of his thirty-sixth birthday. There were 33,000 fans at Ebbets and at one point, they darkened the lights and had everyone light up matches to celebrate Pee Wee. It was quite a sight.

I mentioned the "Mad Monk," Russ Meyer, before. Monk was a real character. He got his nickname deservedly. There were not too many other players in baseball who had a worse temper than he did. But he was also a pretty darn good pitcher when he was under control. He won 15 games for the Dodgers in 1953 and 11 in 1954 and was projected to be in our starting rotation at the start of the 1955 season. At least that's what *he* projected.

But as I said, we came out of spring training with a wealth of healthy starting pitching—Newcombe, Erskine, Loes, and Podres. And only because lefty Karl Spooner—who'd broken in with a sensation in the final week of the 1954 season with a 15-strikeout, 3–0 shutout over the Giants—came up with a sore arm did Monk officially get back into the rotation. Alston had used him sparingly in the spring, prompting Meyer to join the chorus of disgruntled veterans asking to be traded.

"Alston only pitches me against Chicago and Pittsburgh," he moaned. "If he doesn't let me have a regular turn, why doesn't he send me where I'll be appreciated."

Monk got to start the fourth game of the season—against Pittsburgh—and hurled a 6–0 shutout. Unfortunately, in a game in Milwaukee on June 26, he was involved in a three-way collision at first base with Hodges and the Braves' Billy Bruton and suffered a broken left shoulder. That took him out of action for nearly six weeks and by the time he got back, Alston had more than enough starters. He did a good job for us in his one stint as a long reliever in the World Series, however, pitching five shutout innings against the Yankees after Spooner was KO'd in the first inning of Game Six.

He started only 10 other games in 1955, four of them against the Cubs and two others against the Pirates in which he was 5-1, so maybe Alston knew what he was doing after all. I believe at one point Meyer had a phenomenal streak of 17 straight wins against the Cubs and at the end of the 1955 season our Dodger statistics people figured out he was 24-3 lifetime against them. The irony of all this is that over the winter, the Dodgers traded him and Hoak to the Cubs for third baseman Ransom Jackson, a deal that didn't sit well with me since I was counting on getting first shot at third base in 1956 after hitting 15 home runs in half a season. In the Cubs' case, I guess it went down as one of those "if you can't beat him, buy him" deals!

There's one other story worth retelling here about the Mad Monk. I only wished I could have been there to see it, but knowing him, I believe it really happened just like everyone said it did over the years. The Dodgers were playing the Phillies on May 25, 1953, in Shibe Park and Monk was pitching with growing frustration over the ball-strike calls of home plate umpire Augie Donatelli. Things came to a head in the fourth inning when Monk stormed off the mound toward the plate. Campy immediately rushed out in front of Donatelli and shooed Monk back to the mound. As he turned and headed back to the mound, Monk heaved the rosin bag thirty feet in the air in a show of disgust, only to have it come down and land on his head! At that point, Donatelli ejected him for throwing equipment and after making his way to the dugout, Monk was caught by one of the TV cameras making an obscene gesture at Donatelli. This, in turn, prompted all sorts of outrage from the Philadelphia political leaders, along with threats that if Monk ever did anything like that again, they'd have him arrested.

When I look back now at that 1955 season, there were so many things about it that didn't really faze me at the time they were happening. I was only twenty-four, a kid who'd grown up in the Midwest, and didn't really know much about all the baseball history in Brooklyn. I never thought about the fact that I won a world championship ring in my first full year in the big leagues until somebody pointed it out to me a few years ago. So Jeter should know, he ain't the only one in the world to be able to say that. With 15 homers and 50 RBIs, most of them in the second half when Alston had me filling in a lot for Jackie at second base, it turned out to be one of my best

years. I wish it weren't so, but I really had only one better year than
that—1958 when I hit .262 with 17 homers, 14 stolen bases, and 60
RBIs.

The other ongoing issue with the Dodgers in 1955 was the growing concern of Walter O'Malley, our owner, about attendance in
Brooklyn. This was also something I didn't pay much attention to
because it didn't affect the players. But in retrospect it kind of sheds
a different light on all the great things that happened for Brooklyn
that year. When we won our tenth-straight game to start the season,
beating the Phillies and Robin Roberts 14–4, the attendance at
Ebbets Field was 3,874. Imagine that today? Overall, we drew just
over a million fans in 1955 and I can understand why O'Malley felt
he had to have a new stadium. In mid-August, he created a stir by
announcing he was going to transfer seven of our home games in
1956 to Jersey City, adding that the Dodgers would totally abandon
Ebbets Field after 1957. History shows he wasn't bluffing.

Once we got to the World Series, you didn't hear much talk about
all this stuff. It was October as usual in New York, with the borough
of Brooklyn renewing its vows to us, and praying this would finally
be the year.

It sure didn't start out that way, though. The Yankees knocked
Newcombe out in the fifth inning of Game One thanks to a pair of
homers by Joe Collins, and Whitey Ford settled down after a shaky
start to hold on for a 6–5 victory. In Game Two, Tommy Byrne went
all the way for the Yankees in a 4–2 win that was settled when they
scored all their runs off Billy Loes with two outs in the fourth inning.
We went back to Brooklyn thankfully unaware of the fact that no
team had ever come back from an 0–2 deficit to win a seven-game
World Series. In fact, I have to confess, nearly fifty years later, I still

never knew that until an old Dodger fan from Brooklyn told me at an autograph show.

We got back into it and put ourselves on the verge of winning the Series by winning Games Three, Four, and Five in Brooklyn. Podres pitched a nifty complete game 7-hitter in the third game. Labine and Bessent turned in five innings of excellent relief work in the 8–5 fourth game, and Duke hit 2 homers in the 5–3 fifth-game win. Remember how he'd told Pee Wee at the end of August he could turn the Ebbets Field boos to cheers with one swing of the bat? Well, Duke put on quite a show in the Series, hitting .320 with 7 RBIs and a record 4 home runs. This was the Duke we'd seen the first four months of the season.

But when the Series went back to Yankee Stadium and Ford beat us on a 5–1 4-hitter in Game Six, I'm sure there was plenty of worry and despair in Brooklyn. It was coming down to Byrne, the veteran lefty who'd handled us pretty good in Game Two, and my running mate, Podres, who was only twenty-three and whose 9-10 record during the regular season, I felt, still qualified him as a full-fledged member of the humpties club. Podres and I have been the best of friends for over fifty years and spent many a time together at the racetrack. We still look back and laugh at the time we lost our entire paychecks at Roosevelt Racetrack and had to borrow a dime from the toll collector to get home.

Fortunately, Johnny didn't know the first thing about pressure, even seventh-game-of-the-World-Series-in-Yankee-Stadium pressure. He was nothing short of magnificent that day, although, as I've so often told everyone, the Dodgers could not have won that World Series without me. And I mean that literally. For if Alston hadn't had the foresight to get me out of the seventh game in the sixth inning, there wouldn't have been any Sandy Amoros to make that game-saving catch in left field off Yogi Berra.

It was a master stroke on Alston's part. Podres was nursing a 1–0 lead into the sixth when we tacked on another run on Hodges's bases-loaded sac fly. Another walk to Hoak loaded the bases again and here Alston elected to go for the big inning by sending up his best pinch hitter, George Shuba, for *me*. Well, Shuba grounded out to end the inning and, for his defensive changes, Alston moved Jim Gilliam from left field to second, where I'd been playing, and inserted Amoros, the bubbly little Cuban, in left.

The play that won the World Series for us was set up when the first two Yankees in the sixth reached safely off Podres—Billy Martin on a leadoff walk and Gil McDougald, who beat out a bunt. Then Yogi hit a ball deep into the left field corner and if the right-handed Gilliam had still been out there, the ball would never have been caught. But Amoros, who was both fast *and* left-handed, was able to just about catch up to the ball before reaching out with his right glove hand and snatching it in the webbing. What is often forgotten is that he then alertly turned and threw to Pee Wee, serving as a cut-off man in shallow left, who fired over to first to double-up McDougald. After that big reprieve, Podres shut the Yankees down the rest of the way and Brooklyn had itself its first-ever world championship.

We all loved Amoros and had a lot of fun with him. He didn't speak much English, but we'd yell stuff at him in the clubhouse and he'd respond with this huge grin that showed off all his teeth. His major league career didn't last long and afterward he fell upon hard times. Every so often I would read stories about him living in near poverty in Florida, his leg amputated because of diabetes. I know the Baseball Assistance Team took care of most of his medical bills, and he was only sixty-two when he died in Miami in 1992. As far as I know, he never lost that good spirit. I remember reading one of the last interviews he did in which he said: "Everybody talks about my catch, but for me that was not the thrill. It *all* was."

I can certainly relate to that.

Besides Podres, I was especially happy for Gil, who drove in both our runs in that seventh game. Until then, Gil had always been re-membered for his World Series slump. In the 1952 Series against the Yankees, he was 0-for-21 and when the slump continued in the 1953 Series, a priest in Brooklyn made headlines by telling his parish-ioners: "It's too hot for a sermon today. Just go out and pray for Gil Hodges."

You can just imagine the celebration afterward. After whooping it up in the visitors' clubhouse at Yankee Stadium for an hour or so, we dressed and got on buses that took us back to Brooklyn where Mr. O'Malley had put together a big party at the Bossert Hotel, which was just a couple of blocks away from the Dodger offices at 215 Montague Street. I'll never forget the sight of the crowds of people hanging out of their apartment windows and lining the streets, cheering, waving Dodger pennants and throwing confetti at us as our buses went by.

The party was catered by Gene Leone, the proprietor of the fa-mous Mama Leone's restaurant in Manhattan. There were lobsters and steak and champagne and open bars everywhere in the room, and the party went on all night. In the middle of it all was Podres, his suit soaked with champagne, and the world—or at least the Brook-lyn part of it—his oyster. *Sport Illustrated* even made him their "Sportsman of the Year" for 1955. I figured they must not have both-ered to take into account our racetrack losses that year.

# CHAPTER 7

# Just Keep It Close, Fellas, and I'll Think of Something

I never dreamed I'd be in baseball so long they'd have to invent jobs to keep me in the game. Maybe that's not exactly right, but I will say this, before I got a call from Butch Hobson (who was then managing the Red Sox) asking me if I'd like to serve as his bench coach in 1992, I'd never heard of that term. I wound up being a bench coach for the next twelve seasons of my career—for Hobson, Don Baylor in Colorado, and finally Joe Torre.

Then, in January of 2004, I got a call from Vince Naimoli, the owner of Tampa Bay Devil Rays, asking me if I'd be interested in coming to work for them on Lou Piniella's staff in a position that he described as being some coaching, instructing, player evaluating, and public relations work with the ballclub. When I told him that working with Lou had a great deal of appeal to me—especially since I didn't want my career to have ended on the sour note it had with the Yankees—Vince put out his hand and said: "Good, now we have to give you a title. How does 'senior adviser' sound?" Well, that sounded just fine to me, although I had to confess this was *really* a new baseball term to me.

It had taken me ten years to figure out what exactly a bench coach does, but once I got with Joe and the Yankees with all those national TV appearances that came with being in the postseason every year, I got the knack of it. Whenever there's a successful double steal, or a pinch-hitting assignment that works, you know instinctively the camera is going to zoom in on the manager in the dugout. In those instances, it's the bench coach's job to make sure he's sitting right there next to manager, nudging and slapping him so it looks like the play was your idea. On the other hand, if a guy gets thrown out trying to steal, or your pitcher gives up a home run, the camera will also pan on the manager and, in those cases, the bench coach has to know to get up immediately and head down to the end of the dugout to the water cooler so as not to be implicated with the manager.

It's probably going to take me awhile to figure out how to make a senior adviser look just as indispensable!

Meanwhile, I've often been asked what has been the most enjoyable part of my baseball career. Well, obviously, I've enjoyed everything I've ever done in baseball, but the best part of it has to have been the playing because that's really what it's all about. I wish I could have played a lot longer than I did, but when your batting average drops below that .200 "Mendoza line"—as mine did with the Washington Senators in 1965—this is more than sufficient grounds for having your services no longer wanted.

After playing, however, managing is a close second in terms of enjoyment, if only because of the challenges that go with it. When you're the manager, you're the "out front" guy for the whole organization. You make the decisions that are supposed to affect the winning or the losing of a ballgame. Somebody once said that managers get too much of the credit for the team winning and too much of the blame when it loses, and I would have to agree with that. The players ultimately decide a manager's fate by how they execute his decisions.

A prime example of that is what happened to my good friend Gene Mauch in 1986. First of all, let me say this: Gene was maybe the smartest manager I was ever around. When people challenge me on that by saying, "What did he ever win?" my response is: "How many years did he manage?" The answer is twenty-six years. Only four managers in the history of the game—Connie Mack, John McGraw, Bucky Harris, and Sparky Anderson—ever managed as long or longer and they're all in the Hall of Fame. So even though "Number Four"—that's what I always call Gene—never got to a World Series, he must have done something right to have managed all that time.

In 1971, I'd spent four years managing in the minor leagues and I really believed I was ready to manage in the majors. But the team I was working for at the time—the San Diego Padres—wasn't ready to bring me to the big leagues, and then I got a call from Mauch to come coach third base for him with the Montreal Expos. In just that one year of coaching for Mauch, I learned more about managing—how to think ahead in games, the importance of really knowing your players, and more—than from anyone I've ever been associated with in baseball. He was ahead of everybody else during a ballgame and he never got caught short at the end. That's why I think I probably never hurt so much for a man as I did for Mauch in the 1986 American League Championship Series.

Mauch was managing the California Angels against the Red Sox and he'd had this World Series monkey on his back ever since 1964 when his Philadelphia Phillies, a team that had overachieved all year for him, blew a 6½-game lead with 12 to go. He'd come even closer in 1982 with the Angels when he won the American League West, but lost to the Milwaukee Brewers in a best-of-five ALCS. So in 1986, he was ahead three games to one on the Red Sox and the Angels took a 5–2 lead into the ninth in Game Five in Anaheim. At one point during that inning, Mauch was *twice* one strike away from going to the World Series, but he never got it, and not by any fault of his own. His starting pitcher, Mike Witt, had pitched a brilliant game up to that point, the only runs off him being a 2-run homer by Red Sox catcher Rich Gedman in the second inning.

Bill Buckner led off the ninth inning for Boston with a single and one out later, Don Baylor hit a homer to make it a 5–4 game. When Witt got the next batter, Dwight Evans, to pop up to short for the second out, Mauch made his first move. With Gedman, a left-handed hitter, due up again, Mauch brought in his best lefty reliever, Gary Lucas. It was absolutely the right move to make, except that Lucas hit Gedman with his first pitch. That was the first sign that this was a game Mauch just wasn't destined to win. It was the first batter Lucas had hit all season! Now, with the right-handed hitting Dave Henderson coming up, Mauch had to make another pitching change and brought in his closer. Donnie Moore. Again, the only move to make in that situation. I was watching this on TV and I imagined the churning in Gene's stomach, especially after Moore got ahead 1-2 in the count, and got Henderson to foul another pitch off on 2-2. The next pitch was hit over the fence and even though the Angels came back to tie the game in the bottom of the ninth, they lost in extra innings, sending the series back to Boston where they lost Games Six and Seven as well.

I really felt for Gene on that one and it's no consolation to merely sum it up as "one of those games you're just not supposed to win" but it was. Donnie Moore apparently never got over it and, a few years later, committed suicide—a terrible tragedy. But I've always believed there *are* games you're just not supposed to win—another case in point being the Yankees' Game Seven loss to Arizona in the 2001 World Series. In that one, Alfonso Soriano had given us a 2–1 lead with a leadoff homer against Curt Schilling in the eighth inning and Joe Torre brought in Mariano Rivera to close it out in the bottom of the inning. Rivera, who hadn't blown a save in 39 postseason appearances going back to 1997, retired the Diamondbacks in order in the eighth, only to lose the game in shocking fashion in the ninth when he threw Damian Miller's bunt into center field.

After the Diamondbacks went on to score 2 runs, there was actually some criticism of Joe for using Rivera for two innings. I couldn't believe such hogwash! We're talking about the seventh game of the World Series here in which we had the *lead*—it's not like you're saving a guy for tomorrow—especially a guy who'd been infallible in postseason for four years. What did coming into the game in the eighth inning have to do with Rivera throwing a ball into center field? He was one of the best athletes on our club! This was plain and simple a case of the odds finally catching up to us. Nobody can be perfect and, that night, Rivera proved it.

While we're on the subject of using your closer before the ninth inning, in the modern-day age of specialization in baseball, this has suddenly become another no-no in the so-called book. Baseball fans know the expression—"he went by the book there" or the variation "that's a textbook baseball move." But if you ask me, the "book" is nothing more than a safety valve for managers when they have to answer to the media after games for the moves they made.

I'll tell you what I mean. One supposed "no-no" that's been part of the book since time began is: You never put the winning run on base (or, if he's already on base, in scoring position). In a game that decided the National League East pennant race in 1980, Dick Williams, who was managing the Montreal Expos against the Philadelphia Phillies, was faced with this situation and made a decision that, I'd have to guess, haunted him for a long time afterward. Believe me, all managers have these scars to bear.

In this case, the Phillies and Expos were tied 4–4 in the eleventh inning in the next-to-last game of the season. By beating the Expos 2–1 the night before (in which Mike Schmidt drove in both runs), the Phillies had a 1-game lead in the standings. Now, with one out and Pete Rose on first base after a leadoff single, Schmidt was at the plate again. The guy hitting behind him was a rookie catcher, Don McCormack, who had just been called up. The reason he was hitting fourth was because Phillies manager Dallas Green had pinch-run for his two other catchers, Keith Moreland and Bob Boone, earlier in the game.

So Williams had a choice. He could have ordered his pitcher, Stan Bahnsen, to walk Schmidt and take his chances with the rookie, Mc-Cormack, but if he did that, he would be going against the book by putting Rose into scoring position. Bahnsen was a veteran pitcher who'd had some success against Schmidt and I guess Dick was hoping he could get a double-play ball there. In any case, he made the "book" move by pitching to Schmidt, rather than creating a first-and-second situation, and wound up paying for it when Schmidt hit a home run to win the division pennant for the Phillies.

Another book move I've never quite been able to understand is this notion that it's all right to load the bases by intentionally walking a batter with first base open, but not all right to do it if there are runners on first and second. I realize the thinking goes you never want to intentionally put a runner at third base because there are so many different ways to score from there. But if the intention is not wanting to face a particular batter, what difference does it make where the runners are? It's the same outcome—the bases are loaded and you didn't let this particular guy beat you. This is what happened with Bobby Cox in tenth inning of the fourth game of the Yankees-Braves World Series in 1996.

Cox had brought in a lefty reliever, Steve Avery, to start the tenth inning, and after getting the first batter out, Avery gave up a walk to Tim Raines and a single to Derek Jeter. The next batter was Bernie Williams, who had been about our hottest hitter in that series, and hitting behind him was Andy Fox, a utility infielder who'd gone into the game as a pinch runner and a replacement at third for us the inning before. We had only one pinch hitter left on the bench, Wade Boggs, but it didn't matter to Cox that first base wasn't open or that Boggs was a future Hall of Famer with one of the keenest batting eyes ever. It was Bernie Williams he wasn't about to let beat him and, in my opinion, that was absolutely the right move to make in that situation. You never like to load the bases intentionally, but once you decide that your main objective is not to allow Bernie to beat you, it doesn't matter where the base runners are. You don't go away from that objective just because first base isn't open.

Nevertheless, Cox took a lot of heat for that move after Boggs wound up drawing a walk and we eventually won the game. They said he went "against the book" in walking Bernie with runners at first and second. Well, to that I say, if first base had been open and he'd done the same thing, with the same results, would it have then been OK? The second-guessers missed the point.

The reason I say I agree so wholeheartedly with Cox in that situation is because I did the same thing twice in the same game, with the same hitter. It was in late September 1978. I was managing the Red Sox and we were playing the Blue Jays in Toronto. We were five games behind the Yankees in the standings and needed to win just about every game from there on out to have any chance of making the playoffs. Although we ultimately won that one 7–6 in fourteen innings, I believe it very easily could have ended badly twice earlier in the game had I allowed Roy Howell a chance to hit. Howell, the Blue Jays' third baseman, simply ate our lunch. The score was tied in the ninth when he came to the plate with runners at first and second and two outs. The guy hitting behind Howell, Otto Velez, was a pretty good hitter too, so when I put up four fingers, my catcher, Carlton Fisk, looked over at the dugout as if to say, "What the hell are we doing?" My pitcher, Dick Drago, gave me the same look, so now I've got to call time and go out to the mound to explain it to him.

"Howell is not gonna beat us," I said to Drago. "Put him on and just get Velez out."

Drago got the job done that inning, and then in the twelfth the very same situation came up—runners at first and second, two out and Howell coming up. Well, this time I didn't get any funny looks from Drago or Fisk when I ordered the intentional pass again. And luckily we got the same positive result, although not without a little heartburn thrown in for me when Drago went 3-0 on Velez before getting him to pop out.

Now, I'll give you an example of a manager who went *completely* against the book and set himself up for what would have been the all-time second guess. Bottom of the ninth, seventh game of the 1962 World Series. Yankee right-hander Ralph Terry is clinging to a 1–0 lead over the San Francisco Giants. There are two outs, Willie Mays is on second and left-handed Willie McCovey is coming to the plate. The book in this situation says to play the percentages. With first base open, you walk McCovey to face Orlando Cepeda, if nothing else to be able to say you wanted the right-handed hitter against the right-handed pitcher. No one would have ever questioned Yankee manager Ralph Houk for making that move, unless, of course, Cepeda hit a home run. Then they would have said he never should have put the winning run on base.

But Houk chose to completely ignore the book in this situation— and perhaps even put out of his mind the fact that Terry had given up a World Series-winning home run to the Pirates' Bill Mazeroski two years earlier. After talking it over with Terry, he elected to pitch to McCovey—and got away with it, barely, when big Willie Mac hit a liner to Bobby Richardson at second to end the Series. Years later, I know Houk was still being asked about that decision—even though it worked out—and his answer was he just felt McCovey might be a little over-anxious and he feared Cepeda, who hadn't had a particularly good Series, might be due.

In other words, Houk went by his gut, rather than by the book. For the most part, that's the way I managed. I'm not saying the book is total BS. I'm sure the vast majority of decisions I made in thirteen years of managing in the big leagues were essentially "by the book." What I am saying is I always relied heavily on my instincts. I learned a lot, in that regard, from my first manager in the big leagues, Charlie Dressen. Dressen was cocky and daring and liked to play hunches. I loved playing for him, but a lot of others didn't because they felt he took too much credit for himself. "Just keep it close fellas and I'll think of something," was the saying they had for him, but that was because Dressen used the "I" word all the time. I really don't think he meant it that way—that it was all *him* and not the team—that was just the way he talked.

But like everything else in baseball since I was a player, managing has changed dramatically. When I played, players had a lot more respect for the managers. I think the money is probably a primary reason for that. Most managers today make less than a million dollars, which is equivalent to what a good backup outfielder or middle reliever makes. Back in the 1950s and 1960s, before the salary explosion in baseball, managers usually made more than all their players with just a few exceptions. Obviously, I'm prejudiced when it comes to this, but I believe that's the way it ought to be. I never have understood the thinking on the owners' part as far as hiring managers for $300,000 to $400,000 and expecting them to command the respect of players making ten times that much. You can certainly make the case for the manager being the most important person in the whole organization. He's in charge of handling $50 million to $100 million worth of talent, he's the organization's "front man" with the media, and he's the one who has to make the decisions that affect the outcome of every game.

Because the players have so much financial independence today, there's no longer that fear factor that once existed when it comes to the manager. Granted, I was a scrub most of my career and, as such, was always on the lower end of the team's salary scale. But with most every manager I played for—Dressen, Walt Alston, Casey Stengel, Fred Hutchinson, and Gil Hodges—there was no question about them being the boss, and they commanded my utmost respect. (In the case of Hutchinson, who had a notorious volcanic temper and holds the all-time record for over-turned "spread" tables, I would add "fear" as well. There were guys on my 1962 Cincinnati Reds team, which he managed, who were terrified of him.)

What used to be hard-and-fast rules, like everybody traveling together as a team, are now subject to routine exceptions. Many of today's players have their own "time share" jets and, if there's an off-day, they go to the manager and tell him they'd like to fly home. I'm not knocking baseball for this. I'm just saying this is the way it is now. It's a whole new world in baseball.

I remember once sitting in the Yankee clubhouse and seeing Mike Mussina heading out the door with his luggage. I asked one of the other coaches: "Where is he going? Did something happen?" He looked at me and smiled. "Where have you been?" he said. "Mussina only occasionally flies with us. He's got his own deal." Hey, nice work if you can get it, I thought.

Something else that took me a long time to comprehend was how players who aren't in the game aren't in the dugout either! The next time you're watching a game on TV and the camera happens to pan to the dugout, look closely to see how many players are sitting there. You might be surprised.

When I managed, I understood that on cold days early in the season players might want to go up to the clubhouse to get a cup of coffee or just to get warm. But today, with separate lounge areas in the clubhouse and the big screen TVs it's too irresistible for them not to just hang out up there during games. I just can't understand why, on nice summer days, a ballplayer would spend five innings in the clubhouse instead of the dugout. It used to really bother me to see seven or eight guys hanging around the clubhouse lounge when we're in the middle of a ballgame. I would never send a coach up there because the players would get pissed at him and think he was a spy. I'd do it myself. You'd hear this excuse "but I can see the game much better on TV," and I hated that answer.

That's why I got a kick out of what Jack McKeon said a few weeks after he took over as manager of the Florida Marlins in 2003. The team had begun to really turn it around and McKeon was asked what the difference was. He replied that all he'd tried to do was change the players' attitude and approach to doing things. He then cited an incident his second day on the job when he looked around on the bench, saw only a handful of players, and went up into the clubhouse only to find the rest of them lying around watching TV. He said he resolved that situation by pulling the plug.

But as I said, this in-game lounging has been a fact of life in baseball for quite awhile now and despite the embarrassment it can bring to a manager, I doubt if there will ever be a general crackdown on it. Baseball is the only sport where this can happen. In football, hockey, or basketball you can't leave the bench in the middle of a game, only at halftimes or between periods when *everyone* goes into the clubhouse. I remember a particularly embarrassing example of this when I was managing the Cubs in 1989 and we were playing the Mets in late September at Wrigley Field. We were winning the game by 3 runs in the ninth inning when the Mets suddenly staged a 2-run rally with two outs, bringing up the third and fourth hitters in their lineup, Kevin McReynolds and Darryl Strawberry, with a chance to win it. Only when Davey Johnson, the Mets manager, looked down his bench neither of them were there. It turned out they were up in the clubhouse, along with several other players. According to the newspaper reports the next day, Strawberry was completely undressed and had to scramble to find his socks and uniform. He did make it for his at bat and, thankfully for us, struck out to end the game.

Afterward, I was told, Johnson was livid and fined the two players $300 each and ordered them to publicly apologize to the rest of the team.

The next day Davey asked me how I would have handled it. They'd almost had to hold up the game. I told him: "You handled it the only way anyone could. You had every right to be royally pissed."

"It's the most upset I've ever been," Davey told the writers. "Not that I haven't been upset before, but this is the first time it's gone this far. It's something I can't believe. It's beyond me."

It wouldn't be now. But at that time, there was not a general awareness of players leaving the dugout before the games were over and it sure didn't help Davey when Strawberry said: "It happens all the time. Guys are in here watching the last out. I was watching the game on TV. I got out there in time. It was no big thing."

Maybe not to Darryl it wasn't, but it made Davey look like he had lost control of his team, and when the Mets fired him as manager the following May, that was one of the factors they cited.

A similar incident occurred on a team where I was coaching. I'd prefer not to mention here the particular team or the player involved, but trust me, this really happened. It was late in the game and we needed a pinch hitter. Unfortunately, the guy we needed was nowhere to be found. We sent someone up to the clubhouse for him and he wasn't there either. It turned out he was in another room down the hall from the clubhouse where they videotape the games. When we finally found him, he barely got to the plate on time and when he did, it was without his spikes because he didn't have time enough to find them.

You've heard the term "players' manager." I was never quite sure what that meant, other than the fact that I would never want it to apply to me. It seems to me a "players' manager" is a guy who lets the players do what they want. I can assure you, none of those five managers I mentioned earlier who I played for would ever be considered "players' managers." I would have to say, though, to manage today you have to be far more flexible, which I guess means you've got to have a little "players' manager" in you.

And this brings me to another issue, which I just *love*—incentive clauses. I didn't know whether to laugh or cry when I read that Alex Rodriguez received an extra $500,000 for winning the MVP award in 2003 and another $100,000 for making the All-Star team! You ask yourself: How do you give a guy $252 million and then say, but that's not all, if you *live up to that money* we'll give you a bonus?

But, of course, most of the players today have these incentives clauses in their contracts—I will say the Yankees are the only team I know that refuses to give them—and as a manager you're frequently put in a difficult position when your priority of winning a ballgame interferes with one of your players reaching a performance bonus plateau. When I was managing the Cubs, I told my general manager, Jimmy Frey, I didn't want to know who needs 50 innings for a $20,000 bonus or 200 plate appearances or whatever. I told him: "I want to be able to manage this team the way I want to manage."

Jimmy agreed and I never knew anything about any of my players' clauses until one day I'm sitting there in the dugout and Luis Salazar, my third baseman pops up to the infield, comes back to the dugout and five guys go up to him and start shaking his hand! I say to myself: "What the hell is *this?*" The next inning, Salazar comes in off the field, sits down next to me, pats me on the shoulder and says, "Thanks a lot, Skip! That was my 300th at bat last inning and I got a nice bonus coming now." Apparently, he'd told his teammates, but I had no idea.

The reason I'd told Frey I didn't want to know about these clauses was because I remembered a bad experience I'd had in 1976 when I was managing the Red Sox. My second baseman that year, Denny Doyle, had been very instrumental in helping the Red Sox get to the World Series the year before. I was a coach in 1975 but became manager in 1976 when the Red Sox fired Darrell Johnson. Now Denny Doyle wasn't nearly the player he'd been the year before (his average had dropped nearly 50 points) and, with 20 games left in the season, we were out of the race and I wanted to start taking a look at young players who might be able to help us the next year. Well, apparently word got back to Doyle that I was planning on having a kid brought up from Pawtucket to play second for the rest of the year and he came to me and said he needed so many more at bats to get his bonus.

I said: "Pal, I feel bad for you, but I want to see this other guy play."

It wasn't the answer he wanted to hear and he was pretty upset. But the next day, to his credit, he came back into my office and said: "I just want to apologize. I put you in a bad situation and I thought that wasn't right."

One other bonus clause situation I got to witness—admittedly with humor—was in 1983 when I was third base coach for the Yankees under Billy Martin. In August of that season, the Yankees made a trade with Pittsburgh for center fielder Omar Moreno. Because Billy was not consulted on the deal, he immediately took a disliking to Moreno. Then, through a writer, Moss Klein of the Newark *Star-Ledger,* Billy found out Moreno had a bonus clause in his contract that paid him $214.29 for each at bat. That's all Billy had to hear. From that day on, he started pinch-hitting for Moreno whenever he could, each time bragging: "Cost him another two hundred!"

Actually, I can understand incentives clauses for backup players or players coming off injuries. It makes sense for clubs to want some assurances the player is going to get into enough games to justify his salary. But to give these bonus clauses to the high-salaried players like A-Rod, in my opinion, is just plain idiotic. Then again, you can't blame today's players for taking what the owners seem so willing to give them. Hell, I'd have loved to have had all these things when I was a player.

When I think back, I wonder how Earl Weaver dealt with incentive clauses. I liked Weaver—we managed against each other in the American League in the 1970s and 1980s when he was with Baltimore and I was with the Red Sox and Rangers. The one thing people always said he was noted for—other than hating the sacrifice bunt—

was the index cards he kept on all of his hitters. As an opposing manager, I didn't know anything about them, but apparently each card had his hitters' lifetime statistics against all the different pitchers. I'd heard how Don Baylor—who played his first four seasons in the majors for the Orioles—used to complain about coming to the ballpark ready to play only to have Weaver call him into his office and say, "Sorry, Donny, the cards got you today." Imagine telling that to a guy who needed his four more at bats for a $5,000 bonus!

There was one favorite story that people used to tell about Weaver and Pat Kelly, one of his outfielders who was also the team leader with the Baseball Chapel. Kelly came up to Weaver after hitting a home run one time and said: "The Good Lord was looking out for me on that one," which prompted Earl to shoot back: "Oh yeah? Well what about the poor sonofabitch on the mound who threw you the high slider? We better not be counting on God. I ain't got no stats on God!"

Weaver was one of the best managers I ever managed against and he's deservedly in the Hall of Fame. I also think it's safe to say he was anything *but* a "players' manager." Mark Belanger, the Orioles' longtime Gold Glove shortstop, once said of Weaver: "Earl's door is open all the time and he'll listen, but in any event he's always right." You frequently heard a lot of grumbling by the Oriole players about Weaver but the testament to his managing ability was that they played for him.

I think of Weaver and Sparky Anderson and Mauch and all the other great managers I've been around and I know there were hundreds of times in their careers when they made the wrong pitching move—or rather the pitching move that didn't work out. A really good manager, after all, is still going to lose 60 to 70 games a year.

The key to success the way I see it is to limit those moves on national TV. This is why I have a lot of empathy for Grady Little.

Since I've been there and done that, I would have to say there's no tougher town to manage in than Boston. The fans there are as knowledgeable as you'll find anywhere in America, but they're also the most frustrated. As in eighty years of frustration. There's an unofficial Baseball Hall of Infamy in Boston filled with fans' villains from over the years who played a part in Red Sox heartbreak—and I'm probably one of 'em. When Bucky Dent hit the homer for the Yankees in the 1978 playoff game, he became an instant immortal as an enemy of the state with Red Sox Nation. But I was the manager who had to watch, disbelieving, as that ball flew over the Green Monster. The 13½-game lead we lost was all anyone talked about in Boston until their next frustration in 1986 against the Mets. No one ever remembers the eight straight games we won at the end of 1975 to force the playoff, which, to me, was the real measure of that team.

But it goes with the territory, and in 2003 Grady Little arrived at that same territory when he decided to leave Pedro Martinez in to pitch in the eighth inning of Game Seven of the 2003 ALCS. I have to admit, sitting in the Yankee dugout and watching David Wells give up the homer to David Ortiz in the bottom of the seventh to make the score 5–2 Boston, I didn't feel so good about our chances coming back. But then after Pedro popped up Nick Johnson to start the eighth, Derek Jeter doubled, Bernie Williams hit an RBI single, and suddenly it was a 2-run game again and Little walked to the mound.

Although it seemed clear Pedro was starting to lose it, you can't dismiss the fact that he was the Red Sox breadwinner and I'm sure that's exactly what was going through Grady Little's mind as he wrestled with the decision to bring in his lefty reliever Alan Embree, who was warming up, to face our lefty-swinging Hideki Matsui. But you know what? In times like this a manager has to ask himself: Am I going to win or lose this game with my best, or turn it over to at least two relievers?

So Little left Pedro in to face Matsui, and Matsui doubled just fair down the right field line to put runners at second and third with Jorge Posada coming up. Now Little was in the all-time no-win situation. He could have taken Pedro out right there—as the fans were imploring him to do—and if the reliever came in and gave up a hit, they'd have all said, "How could you ever take your best pitcher out of a game like that?" Instead, he left him in and Posada hit a blooper over second base that landed in no-man's land and tied the score.

After it was all over, and we won and Grady Little eventually got fired, I thought: This is absolutely amazing. All year long, all everybody said was what a great job Grady Little had done with the Red Sox. He was a candidate for Manager of the Year! If Pedro had pitched out of that jam—as he's certainly done a hundred times in his career—Little would have been given a three-year contract extension. Instead, all it took was *one* decision and he got fired. I just think that's very unfair. If all of this had happened in a Yankee-Red Sox game in July, or if Bill Buckner had committed that error to lose a ballgame for the Red Sox in July, nobody would ever remember it. But in postseason, everything is magnified.

I once had a similar situation in Boston with a pitcher I left in too long, but fortunately it was in the middle of the season and it didn't get me fired. It was during the 1977 season and my pitcher on this day was a right-hander, Reggie Cleveland, who had great stuff but didn't have the command of all his pitches. As he's coming in from the bullpen to start the game, my pitching coach says, "This guy might throw a no-hitter today. He was *that* good warming up in the bullpen before. He had two hellacious pitches, his sinker and his slider."

Well, the first batter hits a single and right there I say to myself: "So much for the no-hitter." The next batter hits a double to left-center and the two batters after that get hits off the wall. Now I've got to get somebody up in the bullpen. I go out to the mound and Reggie says to me: "I don't understand it, Skip. I've got as good a stuff today as I've had all year."

"I understand that," I said, "but so far you ain't missed a bat."

I went back to the bench and said to my pitching coach: "I know what you told me but they're knocking his tits off."

Wouldn't you know, the next batter hit a line drive right off Reggie Cleveland's tits!

I have no idea what Pedro said to Little, but I have to believe he told him he could get out of the jam. When it's your best pitcher, and he tells you that, you've got to stay with him. Unless, that is, you've got Mariano Rivera—who Little didn't.

As I said before, you can be one of the greatest tacticians in the history of the game, but, today, you live and die and are judged by the decisions you make in prime time. Can you imagine today a manager sacrificing with both his number-three and four hitters— back-to-back? Actually, I can hardly imagine a manager today asking his third or fourth hitter to sacrifice *period*. We're talking *ego* here, as was the case in the famous 1977 incident when the Yankees suspended Reggie Jackson for five games for flaunting a bunt sign from Billy Martin. Those middle-of-the-order hitters don't get paid for bunting and they'll let you know that.

Anyway, in the seventh game of the 1955 World Series, what most people may not remember is that Dodger manager Walter Alston got our second run in that 2–0 win by asking two future Hall of Famers, our third and fourth hitters, Duke Snider and Roy Campanella, to sacrifice!

Here was the situation: Pee Wee Reese led off the sixth inning for us with a single. Even though Snider, the next hitter, had both the speed to stay out of the double play and the power to put one over the fence, Alston ordered him to sacrifice. Duke dropped the bunt down to the right of the mound and ended up safe at first when Yankees first baseman Bill Skowron dropped the relay from their pitcher, Tommy Byrne. Suddenly, it's first and second, nobody out and Campy, our cleanup hitter, is at the plate. In Campy's case, there *was* a distinct chance for a double play if he hit the ball on the ground, which is why, I'm sure, Alston had him sacrifice, too. To his credit, he got the job done and, with the runners moved up, Gil Hodges knocked in Reese with a sac fly to deep right-center. It was not the kind of baseball you'd likely see today, simply because we don't practice bunting enough and the manager doesn't dare ask his number-three or four hitter to sacrifice.

And speaking of number-three hitters you'd never think about asking to bunt, a quick word here about Barry Bonds who, in my opinion, may have changed the game more than any player in history. Bonds is a giant (literally) playing among boys. In 2002, he added to his 73-homer record in 2001 by setting major league single-season records for on-base percentage (.582), walks (198), and intentional walks (68). He also reached base safely in 58 consecutive games, tying the National League record set by my old Dodger teammate, Duke Snider, in 1954. All of this was because opposing managers simply didn't know what else to do with him. He's the one player I've ever known who could seemingly hit the ball out of the park at will and, as such, why would you want to pitch to him? With Bonds, however, we've seen new dimensions to the intentional walk—managers will give him a free pass with no outs and nobody on, or with a man on first and nobody out, and, on one occasion, even walk him intentionally with the bases loaded!

That happened on May 28, 1998, when Buck Showalter, then managing the Arizona Diamondbacks, elected to walk Bonds with the bases loaded and two out in the ninth inning of a game in which he was leading the Giants 8–6, Showalter's reliever, Gregg Olson, obliged, making the score 8–7, and then got Brent Mayne to line out to end the game. Afterward, Showalter explained: "I know it was a little unorthodox, but I just felt it was the best chance for us to win a baseball game."

This immediately sent researchers scurrying to the record books to see when the last time a manager had ordered an intentional bases-loaded walk. They were able to uncover only three other instances in the history of the game—the last one being July 23, 1944, in the second game of a doubleheader when Giants manager Mel Ott ordered an intentional pass to "Swish" Nicholson, who had homered four previous times that day. But I think you'd have to agree, no one, not even Babe Ruth, has done more to drive managers crazy than Barry Bonds. (By the way, the first manager to supposedly ever do it was Clark Griffith of the Chicago White Sox who inserted himself into a game as a pitcher against the old Philadelphia A's and then deliberately walked Napoleon Lajoie with the bases loaded. This was in 1901 and I'm just wondering if anyone accused Griffith of trying to reinvent the game?)

Anyway, between the Bonds factor in the National League, what happened to Grady Little, and all the other aspects of the game that have changed so much, you can understand why I might prefer to leave managing today to the younger guys—McKeon, of course, excluded. I realize the new coaching deal in professional sports seems to be the "geezer movement" in which Joe Gibbs, Dick Vermeil, and Bill Parcells have all come back in the NFL and Lenny Wilkens and Larry Brown did the same in the NBA, and I admit I couldn't help but be flattered if someone asked me to manage again. At the same time, though, this is one "geezer" who is hopelessly old-school ingrained. I'd like to think the game will never pass me by—and being there, on the field and around the players, on an everyday basis, reinforces this because you never stop learning and seeing things you thought you'd never see. But, in retrospect, there could have been no more perfect job for me to do this than bench coach. Until, that is, Vince Naimoli and Lou Piniella came up with senior adviser.

# CHAPTER
# 8

## They Played the Game (The Way It Should Be Played)

**P**robably because I've been able to hang around the game as long as I have, people frequently ask me my opinions on ballplayers past and present. Invariably, I've been asked to make comparisons of players from different generations and my answer is always the same: You really can't do this because players today are so different physically and in a lot of ways so, too, is the playing environment. As I've pointed out earlier in this book, when I played in the 1950s and 1960s, we didn't have any sort of weight training programs that they have today; there wasn't nearly so much travel (my first four years in the majors the westernmost major league city was St. Louis), nor was there as much night baseball.

That said, the game is still played the same and thankfully that will never change. I played with and against probably a thousand players, and I've watched first-hand probably another couple of thousand as a manager and a coach. Lots of people have asked me if I could come up with an "all-star" team of players I played or managed against. I told them that would be next to impossible because there have been so many and I wouldn't want to rate players. I would, however, like to talk about a lot of the players I've encountered over the years who played the game the way it should be played. Some of them were All-Stars, even Hall of Famers, and some of them were just plain journeymen like myself. In all their cases, however, they were players I admired.

But before we get into the "all-Zimmer" team, a word about the Hall of Fame. In my 2001 autobiography (the one for my *first* fifty years in baseball), I talked about three particular players I had managed whom I felt belonged in the Hall of Fame: Jim Rice, Ryne Sandberg, and Andre Dawson. At the time, only Rice was eligible and, while he had done well in the Baseball Writers balloting, he had repeatedly fallen short of the necessary 75 percent for election. Since then, Rice has made only a little progress in the election, while Sandberg and Dawson have come on the ballot and gotten around 50 percent. Now I don't pretend to know exactly what constitutes a Hall of Famer except that I was definitely *not* one—it's all a matter of opinion. But I do think there are certain criteria that make candidates more obvious. For example, it's been pretty much a given if a player has 3,000 hits or 500 homers he's in (although I think, as the years go by, the 500 homers won't be quite so automatic the way the bigger, stronger players are hitting them today). In addition, all the pitchers with 300 wins are in and I'm not sure if, other than maybe Greg Maddux, we'll ever see another 300-game winner. The other criteria, which I've heard the writers cite when they're debating on the Hall of Fame, is dominance—and it's this one where I feel Rice, Sandberg, and Dawson all made their case.

We'll start with Rice. I think if you'd ask anyone who played, managed, or coached in the American League from 1975 to 1986 to pick the most dominant hitter in the league during that period you'd get Jim Rice's name from at least three-fourths of them. Those who wouldn't name him, in my opinion, just weren't watching very closely. In that twelve-year span, Rice drove in 100 or more runs eight times, leading the league twice. He also won three home run titles and four times had 200 or more hits, a rarity for a slugger. He was an eight-time All-Star, hit .300 seven times, and in 1978 as the American League MVP, he had one of the single greatest seasons in baseball history when he batted .315, scored 121 runs, and led the league in hits (213), triples (15), homers (45), RBIs (139), and slugging (.600). I don't know if there was a more feared hitter in baseball in that time, and what isn't often talked about is the fact that Jimmy made himself into one of the better defensive outfielders in the league, especially in Fenway Park, where he'd spend hours taking fly balls off that left field wall until he became a master at playing it.

I'm just guessing here, but if there are two things that have gone against Rice in the Hall of Fame voting it would be his disposition toward the writers and the fact that he didn't have any real big World Series. He was hurt for the 1975 Series, and in 1986 against the Mets he batted what I guess you'd call a quiet .333 because he didn't have any homers or RBIs. More than anything, though, I suspect the fact that Jimmy was never particularly friendly to the writers has hurt him. It's human nature I suppose—and I told Jim this when I managed him in Boston—that it would only be to his benefit if he were more cooperative with the writers. But he was burned once by a writer and I guess he just never could get over it. In any case, I would hope the writers who vote on the Hall of Fame could bring themselves to look past whatever personal differences they may have had with him and judge him by his record on the field. If they do, I think they would have to conclude he more than fulfilled the "dominated the game" criteria.

The same can be said—again in my opinion—for Sandberg and Dawson.

Let's talk about Sandberg. Here was a guy who couldn't have been more dominant at his position. When he retired from the game in 1997, Sandberg held the all-time records for most homers by a second baseman (277), highest lifetime fielding percentage for a second baseman (.989), and most consecutive games without an error by a second baseman (123). As of this writing, he still holds all those records. He won nine Gold Gloves at second base and was named to ten All-Star teams. I mean, if that isn't domination at your position, then what is? Now if there was one thing Ryne Sandberg wasn't, it was a holler-guy. When I managed him with the Cubs, I never even knew he was there half the time, and I told people countless times, what better person could you want on your ballclub? All he does is come to the ballpark and play every day and not give you an ounce of trouble.

Again, I don't know what more the writers could want from Sandberg. He was simply the best second baseman of his time with some records that put him in a class with the greatest second base-men of *all time*. Even though he won a National League MVP in 1984, Sandberg never got the national recognition of playing in a World Series and maybe that's the reason he hasn't been elected to the Hall yet. I have to believe there's something to be said for getting the voters' attention by playing on baseball's biggest stage, but that shouldn't be held against Sandberg. It wasn't his fault the Cubs never got there.

I suspect Dawson may have also been hurt by the fact that he, too, never got to a World Series to display his considerable abilities and that, in his only two postseason appearances, with the Montreal Expos in 1981 and my Cubs in 1989, he picked the wrong time to have a slump. I've always said I never felt worse for a player than I did for Dawson in 1989. He'd been hurt that season, but still man-aged to hit 21 homers with 77 RBIs in just 118 games and played a major role in our winning of the NL East division title. But against the Giants in the National League Championship Series, he just couldn't buy a hit. It was one of those things that can happen to the best of them. People forget now how Barry Bonds, for whatever reason, struggled terribly in his first three trips to the postseason with the Pi-rates, managing just 1 homer and 3 RBIs in 68 National League Championship Series games before he came to the Giants and righted all of that. In 2002, he hit 3 homers in the division series, had a homer and 6 RBIs in the NLCS and capped it off by hitting .471 with 4 homers in the World Series.

Unfortunately, Dawson never got another chance like Bonds, but that shouldn't take away from all he accomplished over 21 seasons from 1976 to 1996. He was an eight-time All-Star, won the NL MVP award in 1987 when he led the league in homers (49) and RBI (137), and finished with 438 homers and 1,591 RBIs. He was also a superb right fielder.

Anyway, that's my case for three good men. I hope when I write my next autobiography fifty years from now I won't have to still be making it.

Now on to some players I got to admire and respect from the other side of the field.

When I was playing, mostly in the National League in the 1950s, there were two opposing players who stood out above all others—Stan Musial and Willie Mays. I've always said Willie Mays was the best player I ever saw, but the longer I watch Alex Rodriguez I'm thinking I may have to eventually amend that. In the spring of 2004 after A-Rod had come over to the Yankees from Texas, there were naturally all the questions about whether he'd be able to make the adjustment from shortstop to third base. To be honest, I thought those questions were kind of silly because A-Rod is simply a natural athlete who, if you ask me, would be an All-Star at any position other than pitcher and catcher. Jackie Robinson was the same way. He'd been a football and track star in college and when he came to the Dodgers, he started out as a first baseman before subsequently making easy adjustments to second base, third base, and the outfield. I respect A-Rod enormously for making the move to third base, at just twenty-eight, in the height of his career as a shortstop. When Jackie moved off second base in 1953, he was thirty-four and he recognized the superior defensive abilities of the up-and-coming Junior Gilliam at second.

Getting back to Mays, I believe he, too, could have been an All-Star at any position. I remember watching him just fooling around taking grounders at shortstop before games. He was so fluid and easy in his movement. Willie once told me: "If you're thinking the game, with my speed, I really don't need to watch." I suppose there's a lot of merit to this because he'd go from second to third, looking backwards and not breaking stride. I couldn't do that. Willie only knew how to play one way and that was all-out, with a flair. I played with him in winter ball in Puerto Rico in 1955 after he'd just hit 51 homers for the Giants. Herman Franks, who was a coach for the Giants under Leo Durocher, was our manager and I remember him saying how refreshing it was to see a guy like Willie playing so hard in winter ball and having so much fun. It's the way you're supposed to play. It takes ability to hit and catch, but not to run to first base all out. Give the fans their money's worth!

This is something I've tried to impress upon Carl Crawford, one of our fine young players with the Devil Rays. Crawford is one of the fastest men in baseball and a natural athlete along the lines of Mays, Robinson, and A-Rod. One day in spring training 2004, he hit a ball to right-center field and kind of jogged out of the box as it dropped in for a base hit. Upon seeing it had dropped, he turned it up as he rounded first and slid into second an instant ahead of the throw. When he later came into the dugout, I said to him: "Carl, it wouldn't have even been a play if you did it like Joe D. or Mays." I had been telling him earlier that spring about what Ted Williams always said about Joe DiMaggio—that Joe was the best base runner he'd ever seen.

"What made him such a great base runner?" I had asked Ted.

"Because," he had answered, "Joe's first two steps out of the box he's running full tilt. He's always thinking of a double."

So I reminded Crawford again of this, and he nodded and admitted his mistake. His greatest asset is his speed and he needs to use that to the fullest. Guys with his speed should always be thinking double. Then again, I never could understand why all players didn't run all-out to first base, regardless of their speed. I remember how annoyed I got at players who would criticize Pete Rose for running to first on a walk. "Charlie Hustle, my ass!" you'd hear them say, to which I'd shoot back: "We should all play the game that way."

While Willie Mays was by far the standout player on the Giants, he had a supporting cast that made them consistently our toughest rivals when I was with the Dodgers. Three players in particular who made a big impression on me when we played the Giants were shortstop Alvin Dark, third baseman Henry Thompson, and the left-fielder, Monte Irvin. Dark, who hailed from Lake Charles, Louisiana, where he was an all-southern high school quarterback, was the Giants' team captain. He reminded me a lot of our own shortstop and captain, Pee Wee Reese, in that they were both quiet, take-charge guys on the field who were not outwardly combative. But do something to one of their teammates, and beware of swift and certain consequences. Dark, I'm sure, took his lead from Leo Durocher, the Giants manager who made him captain. You'd watch over at the Giant bench when one of their hitters got knocked down with a pitch and there would be Dark, walking over to their pitcher that day, whispering in his ear that retaliatory measures were in order.

Although Dark didn't have the greatest range for a shortstop, he became a master at how to play the hitters, and between him and Thompson it was not easy getting base hits through the left side of that Giant infield. "You don't have to make the diving, spectacular plays to be a great ballplayer," he once said. "A great ballplayer is the man who can make the plays within his range and make them consistently." I never forgot that.

It was as a hitter, however, that Dark most impressed me. He batted .289 lifetime, but he was maybe the best hit-and-run man I ever saw. In that respect, the Polo Grounds was built for him, being 260 feet down each line, which forced the outfielders to bunch toward the middle. That, consequently, enabled Dark to pull or push the ball to right or left where there was a lot of space. He was so good at the hit-and-run. Most right-handed hitters get that sign and want to hit the ball to right field. But Dark would always watch who was covering second, and if it were the shortstop, he'd go the other way. I remember once Walt Alston, our manager with the Dodgers, saying to me: "Did you ever see Alvin Dark swing and miss on a hit-and-run? Then why should *any* man cover? As far as I'm concerned, we should just stay flat! If you do it enough times, they'll try to steal the base."

Dark was also an all-around great athlete. Besides being an all-state football player in high school, he was a great golfer who frequently won the baseball players' tournament we used to have every winter. And he, too, could play any position well and, in fact, played second, short, third, and all three outfield positions in 1953 when Durocher was trying to find a place in the lineup for another of my favorite opposing players, Darryl Spencer. Needless to say, it didn't surprise me in the least when Dark went on to a long and successful managing career after his playing days.

Hank Thompson was another one who could play anywhere, and in fact played a lot of center field for the Giants in 1952 when Mays went away to the Army. But he was firmly entrenched at third base for them when I came up in 1954 and was one of the best I ever saw at that position. In 1950, he made the record books by starting 43 double plays at third base, surpassing the mark set previously by

Hall of Famer Pie Traynor. Thompson was a little guy, just five-ten, 173 pounds, but he had deceptive power. I was always amazed at how far he could hit a ball. He hit 129 homers in a nine-year career that was shortened, I think, because of his drinking problems. When he died in 1969, he was just forty-three. I remember Gary Schumacher, the longtime Giants executive, noting with sadness, "the liquor got to his legs" as a player.

Like Thompson, Monte Irvin left his best years in the old Negro Leagues, but even in his mid-thirties when I played against him in the 1950s, he was one guy who, when he was hitting, I'd stop whatever I was doing to watch. Early on in his career, he was a dead pull hitter who modeled himself after Joe DiMaggio. But during the 1951 season he began to use less wrist snap and more arm power and perfected the art of spraying the ball to all fields. He wound up hitting .312 that year and leading the National League in RBIs with 121. Durocher called him the most underrated player in the game and I couldn't disagree with that. Another thing I couldn't disagree with was Monte's contention that he would have hit at least 100 more homers (than the 99 he had in just eight seasons) if he'd played in Ebbets Field rather than the Polo Grounds. I always felt Ebbets Field with its short fences in left and left-center field was the perfect park for me, too. Irvin hit a lot of long balls to center field, but in the Polo Grounds that was nearly 500 feet. I would have loved to have seen him in his prime—they tell me he hit .346 in eleven seasons in the Negro Leagues—but I can tell you, even past his prime, he was the one hitter after Mays we feared the most on those Giant clubs.

The other team besides the Giants that always seemed to be standing in the Dodgers' way to the National League pennant in the

1950s was the Milwaukee Braves. You think of those Braves teams and the names that quickly come to mind are Warren Spahn and Hank Aaron, two of the greatest players in the history of the game. There is nothing I could say here about those two players most everybody doesn't already know. Spahn has more wins than any left-handed pitcher in history and Aaron has more home runs, RBIs, and total bases than any hitter in history. I also thought Aaron never got the credit he deserved for his defensive abilities in right field. He had a great arm and was every bit a complete player. He once said the thing he was most proud of was the fact that he never struck out 100 times in a season—a feat for a home run hitter. But it is the other Hall of Famer on those Braves teams, Eddie Mathews, for whom I had particular respect, if only because he *made* himself a Hall of Famer.

When Mathews first came up in 1952 he was not a good third baseman. One day, he booted a couple balls against us, and Jackie Robinson hollered at him: "Put that glove on your foot!" Well, two years later, he was one of the better third basemen in the game, all because of hard work. He was raw when he first came up, but he could run. In that respect, he was a lot like Musial in that he had deceptive speed for a slugger. He also had good range, but what he needed to develop was his footwork. I remember once hearing Mathews talk about his fielding problems when he first came up and how he corrected them. "When I was playing in the minors I sometimes wished I'd boot grounders so I knew the guy would only get to first base. If I picked the ball up, I figured I'd throw it away. So when I got to the big leagues, I started taking grounders, one after another. I'd have them hit them to me for hours. You do that every day for a couple of years, you'll learn how to play third base, if you live." That should be a lesson for every kid with dreams of playing big league ball: Practice and repetition.

Another guy on those Braves teams who I thought was an equally important player to their success was the catcher, Del Crandall. Crandall wasn't a Hall of Famer by any means—he hit only .254 life-time—but he made himself into an All-Star catcher with his defense and his ability to handle pitchers. In 1954, when Crandall was only twenty-four years old, Braves manager Charlie Grimm made him the team captain. "I don't care how old he is," Grimm said. "Del takes charge on the field. He's always hollering and keeping everyone on their toes. A guy like that means a lot to the rest of the club." Crandall was also a dead pull hitter when he first came up, but some-where along the way he got help with his hitting to the point where he became a real good hit-and-run man.

One of the nicest—and scariest—guys I ever knew in baseball was Ted Kluszewski, a big bear of a man who was one of the great left-handed power hitters of all time. "Big Klu," as we called him, was the man in Cincinnati. He hit 251 homers in ten seasons with the Reds, and with those huge biceps of his, struck fear into the heart of every pitcher in the National League. Off the field, however, he was a pussycat, a kind and friendly sort who, after he retired, became one of the best hitting coaches in the game. Klu knew hitting, too. Looking at him, at six-foot-two, 225 pounds, your initial impression would be that he was a typical free-swinging slugger. Not so. The man almost never struck out, which, to me, is nothing short of phe-nomenal for someone who hit as many home runs as he did. For three straight seasons from 1953 to 1955, Kluszewski hit 40 or more homers and had fewer strikeouts: 40 homers and 34 strikeouts in

1953; 49, 35 in 1954; and 47, 40 in 1955. I think it's safe to say we'll never again see anything like that from a power hitter.

Joe Nuxhall, Klu's longtime teammate with the Reds, reminded me of a time the Dodgers were playing the Reds in Crosley Field and my buddy, Johnny Podres, was pitching for us. "Klu hit one back through the middle," Nuxhall related, "and I swear it hit the little white button on the top of Podres's blue Brooklyn cap. Podres wrenched his knee trying to get out of the way of it, and had to leave the game."

For a while there, it looked like Klu was a sure shot for the Hall of Fame. He hit over .300 in seven of his first eight seasons and had five 100-RBI years in that span. But a slipped disc in his back in 1956 severely curtailed that beautiful fluid swing of his and he was never the same hitter after that. Ironically, it was as a hitting coach that he made a Hall of Fame candidate out of another standout Reds player—shortstop Davey Concepcion—nearly twenty years later. In my opinion, Concepcion is another player who doesn't get near the support he deserves in the Hall of Fame balloting. He was on nine All-Star teams and was the shortstop on four Reds World Series teams, finishing with 2,326 hits and five Gold Gloves. Maybe that's his problem. Three other Reds on those teams—Johnny Bench, Joe Morgan, and Tony Perez—are already in the Hall of Fame, and Pete Rose would surely be there too had he not been banned from the game. When Concepcion first came up, he was a dreadful hitter, batting .205 and .209 in his first two seasons. But then Kluszewski got a hold of him and saw something in his hitting potential.

Essentially, Kluszewski convinced Concepcion to go to a lighter bat and move closer to the plate. "It's the speed of the bat, not how hard you swing, that means the most," he told him, and all of a sudden Concepcion began hitting balls in front of the plate. In 1973, his averaged jumped to .287 and until his final season he never hit below .240 again.

When you think about it, the Reds have had a rich tradition of great shortstops, with Eddie Miller and Roy McMillan before Concepcion and Barry Larkin after him. Miller was before my time, but having grown up in Cincinnati I knew all about him. He played briefly with the Reds in 1936 to 1937, was traded to the Boston Braves where he was the National League starting All-Star shortstop in 1940 to 1942, and then came back to the Reds for five more seasons. He was regarded as the best glove man of his day, leading NL shortstops in fielding five times. It was a tribute to his fielding that he lasted as long as he did in the majors as he hit just .238 in fourteen seasons.

McMillan, who I did play against, was very similar to Miller in that he didn't hit much—.243 over sixteen seasons—but was recognized by everyone as the best defensive shortstop in the National League. He was one of the few players in that era who wore glasses, but they didn't help him with his hitting. As a fielder, though, he was something else. In 1954, he set a National League record for double plays by a shortstop, teaming up with his longtime second base partner, Johnny Temple, for 129. He led NL shortstops in fielding four times, putouts three times, and assists four times, and the Reds were more than able to carry his bat because of the presence of some of the best power hitters in the league at that time—Kluszewski, Gus Bell, Wally Post and later Frank Robinson and Vada Pinson—in their lineup. The statement that maybe best describes McMillan's shortstop ability was what my old pal Gene Mauch said about him: "If you're leading by one run in the eighth inning, you just hope that the next six guys hit ground balls to Roy McMillan." And Joe Adcock, the big first baseman who was later McMillan's teammate with the Braves, said: "Roy was the only shortstop I ever saw go deep in the hole twice in a game and throw out Richie Ashburn." Ashburn was the fastest man in baseball in the 1950s.

McMillan's glove earned him a stay of eighteen years in the big leagues, and it might have been even longer had some over-zealous fan not jumped onto the field and torn McMillan's shoulder out of its socket when he was playing for the Mets in 1966. It happened in Pittsburgh, and the fan ran out onto the field to congratulate Willie Stargell for hitting a game-winning homer. As the fan raced toward Stargell, McMillan, who was then thirty-eight, put out his arm to stop him and got whacked in the elbow. A heckuva way to have your career ended, isn't it?

Now on to Barry Larkin, who is the complete package as far as shortstops go and, I have to believe, a Hall of Famer when his time comes. He was an eight-time All-Star from 1988 to 2000, hit over .300 nine times, and won three Gold Gloves. From my standpoint, in fifteen years I never saw a right-handed hitter any better at hitting with a man on second base. It's the little things to help a team win that count most with me and, in those situations, you could always bank on Larkin hitting the ball to right field. You never had to tell him.

By now, you've probably figured out I'm sort of partial to shortstops. I can't help it, having been one myself. I only wish I could've played the way these guys all did. And while I've said you can't compare players from different eras, there's a modern-day shortstop whom I believe is worthy of the Hall of Fame but has had the misfortune of playing in the wrong era. I'm speaking of Omar Vizquel of the Cleveland Indians, the latest in a long line of great shortstops to come out of Venezuela—Chico Carrasquel, Luis Aparicio, Concepcion, and Ozzie Guillen, to name just four of them. Throughout the 1990s, I know there wasn't a better defensive shortstop in the American League, and as his career kicked in, Vizquel turned into a formidable top-of-the-order offensive player with his speed and ability to make contact. I know against the Yankees he was always one of the toughest outs in that Cleveland lineup that included Manny Ramirez, Albert Belle, and Kenny Lofton.

Unfortunately, the five-foot-seven Vizquel got overshadowed by the emergence of A-Rod, Derek Jeter, and Nomar Garciaparra, all of whom brought new dimensions—size and power—to what once was regarded as a primarily defensive position. But when it comes to just playing the position, I don't know if I've ever seen anyone play it better than Vizquel.

Another pint-sized shortstop I greatly admired was Freddie Patek, the five-foot-five pest who played for the Kansas City Royals in the 1970s when I was managing the Rangers and the Red Sox. I remember once seeing him hit 3 home runs in Fenway Park and saying to myself: "Where the hell did all that power come from?" It seemed every time Patek would do something big in a game, the papers would describe him as "Little Freddie Patek" and it got so I wondered if maybe "Little" was really his first name. I only know the guy came up big for a long time. Besides being an excellent shortstop, he stole 30 or more bases eight straight seasons and once led the American League in triples. Little Freddie was your classic underdog and the thing I'll probably remember him most for was the picture of him sitting in Yankee Stadium all alone on the Royals bench, his head buried in his hands, after Kansas City lost the American League Championship Series to the Yankees for the third straight year.

Those Royals teams of the 1970s and 1980s were fun to watch. They were tailor made for that carpet in Royals Stadium. Besides Patek, they had speed guys up and down the lineup like Willie Wilson, U. L. Washington, and Amos Otis. Otis, especially, was a guy I always wished I'd had on my team. I can still see him now, hitting those line drives spinning around in the right field corner as he's sliding into third base. He was an excellent glove man in center field with an above average arm and, believe it or not, there were comparisons made with Joe DiMaggio because of Otis's similarly effortless manner of running down fly balls.

Of course, when you're talking about the Kansas City Royals of the 1970s and 1980s, the one player who epitomized those teams was George Brett, the only man to win batting titles in three different decades. Brett, to me, was the ultimate baseball gamer. How I loved watching him play the game! I'm almost ashamed to admit my role in the famous "Pine Tar Incident" in July of 1983 in which he had a go-ahead and potential game-winning homer against the Yankees disallowed—temporarily—because of too much pine tar on his bat. That was when I was serving as Billy Martin's third base coach with the Yankees and, as I watched Brett taking pregame batting practice, I happened to mention offhandedly to Billy that it looked like Brett's bat was in violation of the rule that says you can have only eighteen inches of pine tar up the handle. Well, Brett wound up hitting a home run off Goose Gossage in the ninth inning to come from behind and potentially beat the Yankees that day and Martin protested about the pine tar on his bat. The umpires concurred and disallowed the homer, prompting one of the most famous player rages in history by Brett. But later the American League president, Lee MacPhail, overruled them and ordered the game replayed from the point of Brett's homer. MacPhail's reasoning for overturning the umpires' decision was that the "spirit of the rule" was such that a little extra pine tar wasn't a violation. I always felt MacPhail was dead wrong on that decision (I mean a rule is a rule, isn't it?) and as much as I liked and respected George Brett, his bat was in violation of that rule. Otherwise, I always felt Brett was one of the greatest hitters I ever saw; a guy who played the game hard every day. If I were picking my own team, he would almost have to be my third baseman. I loved everything about him.

But as long as we're on the subject of third basemen now, I have to put a word in here about a guy who was my favorite player when I was growing up in Cincinnati. Grady Hatton is not exactly a household name now, but he was the player I most wanted to be like when I was in high school. Hatton came up with the Reds in 1946 when he was twenty-three years old, only to be denied a full season because of a freak accident in late August of that year. He was rushing down the runway to the dugout when a little girl happened to run in front of him. In order to avoid crashing into her, he stopped short and slid on the concrete, skidding instead into Harold Parrott, the Dodgers' traveling secretary. He wound up suffering a hairline fracture of his knee and missed the remainder of the season.

Fortunately, that mishap didn't deter Hatton from going on to a decent major league career in which he hit .254 over twelve seasons. He spent the next seven years with Cincinnati, primarily as their third baseman. In his first few years there, before I signed a pro contract myself, I watched his style, particularly how he held his glove and handled the position. Then in 1952, the Reds asked Hatton to move from third base to second. Although he did it without complaint, he said later: "Second base is five times harder than third. It's the meanest job in the infield. You've got more plays. You cover first. You handle bunts and you hold your position when somebody's sliding in to break up a double play. The shortstop doesn't have it as tough because he's always looking at the play. A lot of times, the second baseman has the play behind him."

Having played both positions, I couldn't disagree with him. Nevertheless, Hatton led the National League second basemen in fielding that year with a .990 percentage and was named to the All-Star team. For the rest of his career, though, he was pretty much a utility-man, and in 1956, at just thirty-four, he quit baseball and went into the insurance business. Four years later, he came back as a player-coach with the Cubs, but at five-foot-nine and 170 pounds, he had long ago been an inspiration to me because he got the most out of his ability. When he became manager of the Houston Astros in 1966, he talked about how the scouts didn't give him much chance to succeed. "I was an average ballplayer," he said. "I could do a lot of things pretty good, but wasn't outstanding in any phase of the game." I could certainly relate to that.

I mentioned Stan Musial earlier—a man who had abilities I absolutely could *not* relate to. How he got all those hits and generated all that power with that corkscrew stance of his is still beyond me. The way Aaron, Mays, Ted Williams, and Mickey Mantle hit so many homers in the 1950s to get into that exclusive 500 club, I wonder if Musial's accomplishments got somewhat overshadowed. I don't think a lot of people realize how great this man was. He's fourth on both the all-time lists in hits (3,630) and RBIs (1,951) and second to only Aaron in total bases (6,134)! Talk about dominating the game, Musial won seven batting titles, two RBI titles, and was on twenty All-Star teams! But remember when Aaron said his proudest achievement had been never striking out 100 times in a season? The most strike-outs Musial ever had were 46, in his next-to-last season when he was forty-one.

Of course, with the Dodgers we always saw Musial at his absolute best. He turned Ebbets Field into his own private playground, hitting .356 lifetime there with 37 homers. A lot of people don't know this, but that's how he got his famous nickname "Stan the Man." The Brooklyn fans gave it to him, as every time he'd come to bat in Ebbets you'd hear this mutter in the stands: "Here comes that Man again." And before I move on to another couple of St. Louis Cardi-nals, there's one other stat about Musial worth mentioning, if only because it sums up what an absolute class act he was. In twenty-two years in the big leagues, he was never thrown out of a ballgame!

Musial was very proud of his Polish heritage and I remember one time when my old Dodger roommate, pitcher Ed Roebuck, who was also Polish, got a rare base hit (for him) against the Cardinals. As Roebuck stood at first base, Musial strolled over to him, gave him a friendly pat on the back, and said: "Way to go, Polack!"

As I said, when we played the Cardinals, Musial usually took care of business against us all by himself. But two other Cardinal players in the 1950s—one in the Hall of Fame and one who got a lot of con-sideration—you could never overlook: Red Schoendienst and Ken Boyer.

Schoendienst has long been one of my friends in the game and I'm glad I don't have to make a case for him for the Hall of Fame since he's already there. Red was a switch-hitting, nine-time All-Star at second base for the Cardinals. At six-foot-one, he was big for a second baseman and there was nothing flashy about him, but he played the position as well as I've ever seen it played. Every time you looked up it seemed wherever the ball was hit to that side of the infield, he was there. In 1950, he set a National League record for handling 320 consecutive chances without an error at second. Red simply had a knack for knowing exactly where to play the hitters. He got that from knowing his own pitchers and where they threw the ball.

Red was quite a hitter too. He batted .289 with 2,449 hits lifetime and narrowly missed winning the National League batting title in 1953 when he hit .342. Strangely enough, it was a bad eye that prompted him to become a switch-hitter. As the story goes, at Union City, Tennessee, his first minor league stop in the Cardinals' system, Red hit safely eight straight times right-handed when he suddenly shocked his manager by asking to hit left-handed, explaining that, because of a bad left eye, every time a right-hander threw him a curve ball his nose got in the way and he couldn't pick it up. I only know he hit with authority from both sides of the plate and if he really did have an eye problem he sure fooled the rest of us.

Kenny Boyer was one of the finest third baseman I ever saw. He was more laid back than Brett and maybe that was why he never got credit for the player that he was. He wasn't what you'd call a holler guy in the infield. He just played his ass off. He reminded me in a lot of ways of Sandberg and Dawson. He came from a family of thirteen children and two of his other brothers, Cloyd, a pitcher, and Clete, also a third baseman, played in the majors. Kenny played eleven years with the Cardinals, won five Gold Gloves, and was a seven-time All-Star. To give you an idea of what kind of team player and quiet leader he was, in 1957, a year after he'd hit .306 and been named the National League All-Star third baseman and two years after he'd been Rookie of the Year, he volunteered to move to center field to make room for Eddie Kasko, who was an up-and-coming third baseman in the Cardinal system. Fred Hutchinson was the Cardinal manager at the time and I remember years later him telling me how Boyer really showed him something by doing that. "He didn't have to accept the switch since he was already established as the best in the league at third," Hutch said, "but he did it for the good of the ballclub."

The next year, however, Boyer was back at third, and in 1964 he won National League MVP honors when he led the Cardinals to their first pennant since 1946, hitting .295 with 24 homers and a league-leading 119 RBIs. His play at third base looked effortless, so effortless that fans thought he wasn't hustling. Johnny Keane, the Cardinal manager in 1964, got really upset with that and jumped on those who had criticized Boyer. "I knew what he was doing," Keane said. "I knew he was giving his all and I couldn't believe people would think otherwise. There was nobody better in the field."

Boyer played fifteen years in the big leagues and, in 1978, came back to the Cardinals as their manager, replacing a guy named Vern Rapp who had reportedly lost the Cardinal players by having rules that were too rigid. Not long after they fired Boyer in 1980 (ironically because they said he was too laid-back), he developed lung cancer, and to give you an idea of how highly regarded he was in the baseball community, Billy Martin organized a benefit in spring training in Arizona to help defray Boyer's mounting $200-a-day medical bills. In those days, medical expenses for retired players were not covered under the pension plan and, at $50-a-head plus anything more people wanted to contribute, Martin raised nearly $100,000 in one night. Mickey Mantle, Roger Maris, Harmon Killebrew, Frank Robinson, Reggie Jackson, Eddie Mathews, Bud Selig, Gene Mauch, Bob Lurie, and many more were there. Unfortunately, they couldn't save Kenny, who was too sick to attend the dinner, and on September 7, 1982, he died in St. Louis. He was only fifty-one. Just to add to what Keane and Hutch said about him, I really appreciated the way Ken Boyer played. He made it look so easy—too easy, I suppose, to satisfy some people.

Now I guess by this time you're wondering if I ever saw a pitcher I liked. To be honest, it was my nature to hate pitchers. After all, as far as I was concerned they *were* the enemy, and at least a couple of 'em nearly killed me. Once in a while, though, I *did* get a hit. As I was winding down my career in the early 1960s with the Washington Senators, one pitcher in particular I remember was John Wyatt, the chunky little right-handed closer for the Kansas City A's. Wyatt threw really hard, but he was a high fastball pitcher and that was always my pitch. One game I especially remember was June 8, 1964. My manager with the Senators, Gil Hodges, sent me up to pinch hit in the ninth inning and I hit a homer off Wyatt to win the game. What made it special for me was that it kind of overshadowed the 3 homers my teammate Jim King had hit earlier in the game! In that old Kansas City ballpark, Municipal Stadium, the visiting clubhouse was high up on a hill and the next time we came into town, as I was walking up that hill after Hodges had taken me out of the game, some fan yelled out: "Go back in! Wyatt's coming in!"

Of course, when you're a lifetime .235 hitter it means you didn't have a whole lot of success against a whole lot of pitchers, and for every John Wyatt, there were thirty or forty others I didn't hit so good.

Curveballs always gave me trouble and I don't know of any pitcher who had a better curve than Camilo Pascual, unless it was

Sandy Koufax, Bert Blyleven, or Sad Sam Jones (who pitched for the Indians, Cubs, and Giants in the 1950s and 1960s). Back in the 1950s, old Clark Griffith who owned the original Washington Senators, was notoriously tight with the buck and in order to try and compete with the Yankees, Red Sox, and Indians, he was the first owner to tap into Cuba for cheap talent. Back then, the Senators always seemed to have at least two to three Cubans on their roster, but until Tony Oliva came along after Clark died and his stepson Calvin moved the team to Minnesota, the best of them by far was Pascual. A right-hander, Pascual led the American League in strikeouts three times and in shutouts twice and was the breadwinner on those losing Senators and Twins teams.

I faced Sad Sam Jones when I was in the minors at St. Paul and he was pitching for the Indians' Triple-A team in Indianapolis. A couple of years later, when he was traded to the Cubs, the Dodgers were facing him for the first time and I told Campy and Pee Wee: "This guy has a curve you've never seen before." Well, on that day, he hung just about every curve he threw and they gave me the needle. I said: "I guess I'm wrong, although I still don't think so." The next time we faced him later in the season, he struck out about 10 guys. Pee Wee grabbed his head after getting frozen for strike three on one Jones curve and Campy buckled and nearly fell to the ground striking out on another. I just smiled.

One of the absolute meanest pitchers I ever faced was Jim Bunning, who now happens to be a United States senator from Kentucky. Bunning is in the Hall of Fame with 224 wins to his credit, mostly with the Detroit Tigers and Philadelphia Phillies, but he never forgot my first encounter with him in a game in Miami in spring training of 1955. We were both rookies—I was trying to make the Dodgers and he was trying to make the Tigers. My first time up against him I got a base hit. The next time up, he threw one right underneath my chin. It was a kind of "tester" since I always leaned out over the plate, and sent me upside-down in the box. The next pitch I hit over the left field wall. I've been to a lot of golf tournaments over the years at which Jim was the host, and he'd tell that story.

On the other side of spectrum from Bunning was Stu Miller, a skinny (he weighed only about 165 pounds) relief pitcher for the Cardinals, Giants, and Baltimore Orioles in the 1950s and 1960s. Miller didn't throw all that hard, but he was all arms and head action and I couldn't hit him with a snow shovel. In my only All-Star Game, in 1961 as a Cub, I got to witness something people are still talking about—Stu Miller being blown off the mound at San Francisco's Candlestick Park. Now everybody knows about the notorious winds at Candlestick and how they used to roll in from the outfield in the late afternoon. On that day, Miller was on the mound, getting ready to throw a pitch to the Tigers' Rocky Colavito, when the wind whipped in as he began to go into his motion, causing him to fall down. Miller later insisted his feet never moved and that the story got blown (literally) out of proportion as it was retold through the years. I only know it was one of the funniest things I ever saw happen in a ballgame. By the way, he was charged with a balk as the home plate umpire, Stan Landes, said: "I felt sorry for him, but what could I do? He went into his motion and didn't deliver the pitch. A rule is a rule." Tell that to Lee MacPhail.

As I've said, off-speed pitchers and curveballers were the ones who gave me the most trouble. Give me a guy who threw high fastballs and I was usually a happy hitter. That's why I always enjoyed hitting off Robin Roberts, as great as he was. Robbie was primarily a high fastball pitcher and he always threw strikes. There was one, however, Bob Rush, a big right-hander with the Cubs and Braves, who got me out consistently with high fastballs. For some reason I just didn't see the ball too well with him. Rush was a real workhorse, the ace of those Cubs staffs in the 1950s, routinely pitching 230 or more innings in a season.

I remember Mickey Owen, the Cubs catcher, explaining why Rush was so hard to hit despite being essentially a one-pitch pitcher. "His fastball is enough," Owen said, "because you can't get set for it, even when you know it's coming. The reason is that it doesn't break the same way every time. And when it gets a little farther out, it really sails. When I'm catching him, I stay just as loose back there as if I'm catching knuckleballs from Dutch Leonard. With Rush, you've got to keep swinging and hope that the ball won't break that much."

That's what I did, but it never seemed to do me much good.

Another real tough hard-throwing right-hander for me was Dean Chance. I was at the end of my career with Washington in the American League when Chance first came up with the California Angels in the early 1960s. Here's a stat for modern-day pitching fans: In 1964, the year Chance won the American League Cy Young Award with a 20-9 season and a league-leading 1.65 ERA, he tossed 11 shutouts! I'm sure he got our Senators two or three times that year, and to be honest, I don't remember ever getting a hit off him. Chance probably could have been one of the greatest pitchers of all time, but he was a happy-go-lucky, late-night party guy, and after a prolonged hold-out with the Twins in spring training 1969, he blew his arm out trying to rush back into shape too quickly. I lost track of Chance after he retired prematurely in 1971 and then a couple of years ago I read he'd become the president of the International Boxing Association.

For all of his free-spirit ways, though, he was a good guy and, I'm told, a real student of the game. And he had no regrets either about getting such a short count on his baseball career. "With my motion," he said, "I was lucky to get in ten years." Unfortunately, for me, I saw him in his absolute best years, 1963 and 1964, and I didn't find him very funny at all.

Before anyone gets the idea that I really do hate pitchers, let me say right here for the record that some of my best friends—Roberts, Mel Stottlemyre, Sandy Koufax, Don Drysdale, Roger Craig, Johnny Podres, Ed Roebuck, Jim Kaat, Joe Nuxhall—happen to be pitchers.

I had the privilege of watching almost all of Jim Kaat's distinguished twenty-five-year career from the other side. "Kitty Kaat" is a student of pitching and that served him well in winning 283 games in the big leagues. He once said, "I'll never be considered one of the all-time greats or even maybe one of the all-time goods, but I am one of the all-time survivors." I really think he's being way too modest because if 283 wins doesn't put you in there with the all-time greats, I don't what does. And if there is such a thing as a "complete pitcher" that's what Jim Kaat was too. He hit 16 home runs in his career and he holds the record for most sacrifice hits by a pitcher with 134. And lastly, he was quite possibly the greatest fielding pitcher of all time, as evidenced by the 14 consecutive Gold Gloves he won. One of the great joys for me in my eight years as bench coach with the Yankees was seeing Jim on the days he was broadcasting their games and trading baseball stories.

I imagine the fans in Cincinnati feel the same way about Nuxhall, a lefty like Kaat who after pitching for the Reds for fifteen years, has been telling stories on the radio as the team broadcaster since 1967. I probably have more respect for Nuxhall than any pitcher I've known in baseball simply because of the perseverance he demonstrated during his career. In 1944, when most of the game's best players were still off at war, Nuxhall became the youngest player in National League history when, at just fifteen years old, the Reds signed him and brought him in to pitch in a game in which they were getting blown out by the Cardinals, 13–0. He pitched just two-thirds of an inning, facing the likes of Stan Musial, Walker Cooper, and Marty Marion, and gave up 5 more runs and didn't return to the majors until 1952. But as he once said to me with a chuckle: "I think my record is something that could be broken easier than DiMaggio's 56-game hitting streak."

Jokes aside, the Reds could have really ruined Joe by putting him in that situation. As it was, he spent the next eight years in the minors, in the meantime going back to finish high school, and he had to learn to control his temper which, too often, had gotten the best of him. When he finally did make it back, Nuxhall won 82 games for the Reds between 1953 and 1959. Then in 1960, for unexplained reasons, he just lost it, going 1-8 and being demoted to the bullpen. He was booed for the first time by the Cincy fans to the point where he asked to be traded.

But after a year and a half of finding himself while getting released by three teams in the American League, he came back to the Reds in 1962 and in one of the great comebacks in baseball, won 15 games in 1963. Even though I was over in the American League then, I marveled from afar at Joe's heartwarming comeback story. In recent years, he's had to battle back from a series of health problems, including a second cancer scare in the winter after the 2003 season. But once again he fooled the skeptics, showing up right on time at the Reds camp in spring training, 2004, to take his place in the booth next to his longtime sidekick, Marty Brennaman. Believe me, those two are a couple of real dandies and I only wish I could listen to them every night in my old hometown.

Having given the pitchers their due here, I would be remiss in not mentioning something about the ones who probably annoyed me more than any others—knuckleballers. Despite all the beanings through the years, I was never scared of a thrown ball except a knuckleball, even though it's not thrown hard. The reason is you could never tell which way it was going and with my head, even the softest blow on it could have been a life-threatening situation. So I hated facing knuckleballers—and when I first came up there were a bunch of them in the National League. Hoyt Wilhelm, who was a relief pitcher with the Giants then, was the greatest of them all and the first to be elected to the Hall of Fame. Murray Dickson of the Pirates was another tough one.

If you ask me, though, one of the best knuckleballers of all was Charlie Hough, who wound up pitching twenty-five years in the majors. I managed Charlie with Texas in 1981 and 1982 and what set him apart from so many other knuckleballers was his ability to control the base runners. Because it takes so long to get to the plate, the knuckleball is the easiest pitch to steal on. But when it came to checking the runners, stepping off the rubber, quick-pitching, and all the variations of those things, Hough was as good as there was. Sometimes he'd just hold the ball in getting the runner all jittery.

Even though it's a freak pitch, the knuckleball isn't that hard to master as many a pitcher has picked it up in their later years as a means of prolonging their career. Johnny Lindell, who was a good hitting outfielder with the Yankees in the 1940s, is a guy who had a brief second career as a knuckleball pitcher in the National League. Jesse "Pop" Haines, the Hall of Famer who pitched for the Cardinals in the 1920s and 1930s, was another one who took up the knuckle-ball early in his career and, using it as a second pitch, made himself into one of the best pitchers in the National League. Considering the longevity of knuckleballers, it's a wonder there are so few of them around the game today. I know, for example, the Yankees had more trouble with Tim Wakefield than they did with Pedro Martinez—at least on days when Wakefield's knuckleball was working, and it usually was against us. I guess there's just no glamour in being a knuckleballer. I sure could have done without them.

I know I've said here I don't like to pick All-Star teams, but I am very proud of the fact that, in my managing career with the San Diego Padres in 1972 to 1973, the Boston Red Sox, 1976 to 1980, the Texas Rangers, 1981 to 1982, and Chicago Cubs, 1988 to 1991, I got to manage three Hall of Famers (Carl Yastrzemski, Dave Winfield, and Carlton Fisk) and at least three other players (Greg Maddux, Rafael Palmeiro, and Ryne Sandberg) who I believe are certain to be Hall of Famers. Position by position, here are some of the best play-ers I ever managed in the years I managed them:

CATCHER: Carlton Fisk (Red Sox, 1976 to 1980)

FIRST BASE: Rafael Palmeiro (Cubs, 1988)

SECOND BASE: Ryne Sandberg (Cubs, 1988 to 1991)

SHORTSTOP: Rick Burleson (Red Sox, 1976 to 1980)

Shawon Dunston (Cubs, 1989 to 1991)

THIRD BASE: Buddy Bell (Rangers, 1981 to 1982)

OUTFIELD: Carl Yastrzemski (Red Sox, 1976 to 1980)

Dave Winfield (Padres, 1973)

Jim Rice (Red Sox (1976 to 1980)

Fred Lynn (Red Sox (1976 to 1980)

Andre Dawson (Cubs, 1988 to 1991)

PITCHER: Greg Maddux (1988 to 1991)

I don't know about you, but I'd go to war with this team any day.

But let me also say this: The guys on this team who made it to the Hall of Fame didn't need any help from me. I was just privileged to be a part of their careers. Fisk was already a two-time All-Star when I took over as Red Sox manager in 1976, but for me he was an All-Star three more times and had one of his finest seasons (of the twenty-four he put in) in 1977 when he batted .315 with 26 homers and 102 RBIs. Palmeiro was a baby when he played for me in my first season as Cubs manager in 1988. He made the All-Star team that year, batting .307, but to show you what a great evaluator of talent I am, we traded him to the Rangers after that season for closer Mitch Williams. Jim Frey, my boss, came to me with the trade proposal that winter, and as much as I loved Palmeiro's swing, I told Jim I just didn't think he was ever going to hit for power. Some 500 homers later, I guess Palmeiro's pretty much dispelled that notion!

I've mentioned how Sandberg holds the all-time records for home runs and fielding percentage for a second baseman. Rick Burleson was an All-Star shortstop for me in Boston in 1979 and two years earlier had his best season in the majors, hitting .293 with 52 RBIs. I loved his gritty approach to the game. Shawon Dunston had maybe the strongest throwing arm of any shortstop I ever saw. He was still coming into his own when I took over as Cubs manager in 1988 and he made the All-Star team that first year with me, and again in 1990. He was still playing as of 2003, having accumulated more than 1,500 hits.

I had the privilege of knowing Buddy Bell's dad, Gus, very well and we played together briefly with the Mets in 1962. Gus Bell hit 206 homers in the big leagues, but Buddy was an even better player. A five-time All-Star third baseman, Buddy had two of those seasons for me in Texas.

As for my outfield, I had Yaz at the end of his career and Winfield at the very beginning of his. They're both members of baseball's select 3,000-hit club. That Padre team I managed in 1973 was not very good and I had to argue with my boss, Buzzie Bavasi, to let me keep Winfield, who was a number-one June draft pick that year. Buzzie wanted to send Winfield to the minors for some seasoning, but I took one look at this physically gifted, six-foot-six athlete who had a cannon of an arm and could run like a deer and I knew it didn't matter how young or inexperienced he was. He was going to be better than anyone I had, and he was. Just a great, great, complete player.

I've talked about how Rice, in 1978, had for me one of the greatest seasons of any hitter in the history of the game, but when he came up in 1975, I didn't think he was going to be better than Fred Lynn, who was a fellow rookie on the Red Sox that year. Lynn was a guy who could also do it all—run, throw, hit, and hit for power—and in 1975 he won both Rookie of the Year and MVP honors. For me, in 1979, he had a phenomenal season, winning the batting title with a .333 average, hitting 39 homers, scoring 116 runs, and knocking in 122. But in 1981, a contract dispute led to the Red Sox trading him to the California Angels and, for some reason, he was never the same player.

I had Maddux at the very beginning, too, and while he didn't start winning all his Cy Young awards until after I got fired in Chicago, I got to see his development into a great pitcher. He went through a lot of growing pains in 1987 when he was 6-14. But that winter Maddux did a lot of soul searching and learned how to study hitters and how to pitch to them. Maddux is one of the real students of the game. And that, more than anything else, is what sustained him to a likely Hall of Fame career. In 1988, he was 18-8 and never had a losing season again.

As I feared, I know there are a lot of players I failed to mention here that played the game with the same passion, determination, perseverance, and smarts as these. You like to think you batted 1.000, but to those I forgot, all I can say is, what can you expect from a lifetime .235 hitter?

# CHAPTER

## 9

Soot:
A Baseball
Wife

I t sure has been a long and wonderful baseball journey for me, seven decades of thrills and fun with (thankfully) only a little bit of tears and pain thrown in. From the upstate New York minor league bus towns of Hornell and Elmira, to the bustle and passion of long ago Brooklyn, across the country to Hollywood, and the later-on separate tours of duty in two of the most treasured ballparks on earth, Wrigley Field and Fenway Park, it always seemed that no matter how far I traveled, I was coming home again, whether it was

Chicago, Boston, New York, or now Tampa Bay. We're talking about a lot of packing and unpacking here, and I am here to say I never had to do any of it. When people talk about how ballplayers are pampered and spoiled? Well, nobody has been more pampered and spoiled than me.

There is a woman I want to talk about now who has been there by my side through every step of this journey, making sure I got to wherever I was supposed to be. Her name was Jean Carol Bauerle when I first met her at Western Hills High School in Cincinnati in the late 1940s, but in the fifty-three years we've been married, she's been known as Soot to everyone. I agree, it's a strange nickname and I don't know how many times people would very cautiously ask me if it had something to do with her having a dirty face when she was a little kid. The fact of the matter is, the "Soot" is what I suppose you'd call a derivative of an affectionate term used by her grandmother who was of German descent. "My little 'Soot-a-la'" is what her grandmother always called her as she doted on her, and through the years everybody kind of picked up on that and it got shortened to "Soot." Nobody ever called her Jean. As far as having anything to do with chimney dust, I can assure you the only dust associated with my wife is the dust I've left behind in all my many stops along the baseball landscape. Believe me, the term "journeyman ballplayer" is not lost on Soot.

She has been my strength and my inspiration and without her I would be nothing. She nursed me back to the land of the living through two critical beanings, and singlehandedly raised our two children, Tom and Donna, while I was always away someplace playing ball. She's my secretary, my bookkeeper, my travel agent, my own "senior adviser" and, above all else, my life's partner. My friends have told me that being married to me and putting up with all my trials and tribulations has guaranteed Soot a place in Heaven, right there with all the other Saints. I don't doubt that in the least. Saint Soot. It even *sounds* right! But then, you probably need to hear her side of the story, which is why I'm now going to turn the rest of this chapter over to the ultimate baseball wife.

## SOOT'S STORY

We met at Western Hills High School where we were both in the same class. It was our junior year and Don was the star quarterback on the football team and I was a member of a sorority. We were having a hayride and some of my friends said, "Oh you, you've got to go!" But if there was one thing I hated about those things was that we had to do the asking. We were standing in the hallway and Don happened to be a few feet away talking to a bunch of guys. I noticed him but I had never been formally introduced to him. As such, I didn't want to personally go up to him and ask him to the hayride for fear of being turned down, so one of the guys standing there said: "I'll go over and ask him so you won't be embarrassed." Well, unbeknownst to me, Don told him no. But when the guy came back, he said to me: "Just go ask him!" So I went over to him and everybody's standing around laughing. I said to him: "Everybody knows what I'm going to ask you. Will you go to the hayride with me?" and wouldn't you know, he said yes!

We started dating from that point on and then shortly after graduation, he went away to play ball in Cambridge, Maryland, for $150 a month, and I went into nurse's training. He wasn't happy about my getting a job. We had already agreed we were going to get married and he said: "No wife of mine is ever gonna work!" Well, two years later, Don was playing in Elmira, New York, and he had a roommate, Ed Roebuck, who was also engaged, and they started talking about getting married at home plate. We were both under twenty-one, so we needed our parents' permission to get married. My parents had no problem with the home plate thing, but they said, "We'll give our permission on the condition that you finish your nursing classes."

So I had all my papers transferred from Christ Hospital in Cincinnati to the hospital in Elmira and we got married, without the Roebucks, who decided they wanted to get married in a church. Immediately after the home plate ceremony, Don changed out of his white Palm Beach suit and played in the game, and I went up in the stands to watch, still wearing my wedding dress. At the end of the season, I had ten months to go in my three-year course and Don got an offer to play winter ball in Caracas, Venezuela. Well, here we were, two kids from Cincinnati, and this sounded like "wow!" My mom and dad said we might never get this opportunity again, and they didn't hold me to the promise that I'd finish nursing school.

But there were extenuating problems that we hadn't counted on. Don was 1-A and had to report to his draft board. When he got down there, they told him: "You're not going anywhere, but to get a physical and from there you'll probably be going overseas." That was when the war in Korea was on. So that put an end to the Caracas thing. Instead, we took a belated honeymoon to Florida. After that, we came back to Cincinnati and Don reported to the draft board for his physical. It turned out he had one bad eye, a lazy eye as they called it, which he knew about. Nevertheless, he cheated on the eye test to pass it because all his buddies were going into the Marines and he wanted to go with them.

He probably would have, too, except now that became complicated by the fact that *I* became pregnant. In those days, the rules were if you were married and your wife was pregnant you had to be reclassified 3-A. I had my doctor write a letter and Don was given a deferment as all his buddies went off to the Marines.

By now, though, it was too late for the Caracas trip, but later that winter, Al Campanis, who was heading up the Dodger scouting department, called Don and told him they needed a shortstop for the Cienfuegos team in Havana, Cuba. Here we were, in the dead of winter in this little apartment in Cincinnati, and I was pregnant and Don said to me: "Do you want to go down there?" I said: "Are you kidding?" It was cold and miserable in Cincinnati, and we flew out of there to Miami where everybody was in their shorts and from there we flew to Havana, and I'll tell you, we felt we were in paradise!

The following spring training we were supposed to go to Mobile, Alabama, for the 1952 season. Don came home to Cincinnati from Vero Beach for a couple of days and we packed up our car, me pregnant with Tommy, and drove all the way to Alabama. Then, in 1953, we did the same routine only this time to St. Paul. During that season, when Don left on a road trip to Columbus, I found out I was pregnant again, with Donna. The radio in our apartment was broken, so I couldn't listen to the games. As I sat there one night, one of the other players' wives in the complex came running over, screaming: "Soot! Soot!" I couldn't imagine what she wanted. "Don just got beaned!" she yelled. With that, she brought her radio over and I sat there with her, and as I listened to the broadcasters I could tell by the way they were talking it was serious. The next thing I knew, I got a call from somebody with the team telling me I should make arrangements to fly to Columbus.

Here I was, I had a toddler, Tom, and nobody knew I was pregnant with Donna, and my husband was lying in a hospital 800 miles away in critical condition. I left Tom in St. Paul with Velma Lindsey, one of the other players' wives who really loved him, and she took care of him while I went off to Columbus. When I got there, Don's parents were both with him in the hospital, having driven up from Cincinnati. That's when my two years of nurse's training began to pay off. Whenever the doctors would explain all the things that were going on with Don, I was able to understand. Never once, however, did the doctor give us the feeling that he wasn't going to be fine.

Dr. Lefebvre was his name and he was always so positive, I think for our benefit. But the next year when Don went back to visit the doctor for a checkup, he overheard the doctor say to a colleague: "See that young fellow walking down the hall there? Last year I wouldn't have given you two cents he would survive. Only because he was in such good shape and young, was he able to make a complete recovery." I never forgot that, or the way this wonderful brain surgeon had been so reassuring to me. Unfortunately, we learned later he committed suicide because he had some fatal disease. This brilliant doctor who saved Don's life felt he couldn't help save himself. We were crushed when we heard that.

Don was in the hospital for four weeks after the beaning, the first six days in a coma. But at the end of the four weeks as I was talking about all he'd been through (learning all his motor skills again and regaining his eyesight), he looked at me and said: "What are you talking about, anyway? How long have I been in here?" It was like he was just waking up. He'd been awake, but he thought he'd only been in there overnight. Again, I was thankful for my little nursing school training to help me get through that.

This was my rude introduction to baseball, or at least a part of it I never envisioned. It hit home even more when, after that beaning, Dodger general manager Buzzie Bavasi ordered protective liners put in all the players' caps in the organization. Later on, largely because of Don's beanings, helmets became mandatory in both leagues.

We were back in St. Paul the next year where the Dodgers wanted to see if Don was going to be able to regain all his skills. I thought we'd probably be there the whole year when we got the call from Buzzie that Pee Wee Reese had gotten hurt, and Don needed to report to the team in Philadelphia. I figured it was going to be only a temporary stay, but Don had other ideas. He felt he had nothing more to prove at St. Paul and, so, when Pee Wee came back a week later, and Buzzie gave him a choice of going back to the minors and playing every day or sitting on the bench in Brooklyn, Don chose Brooklyn. He went out and found an apartment on Fort Hamilton Parkway and called me in St. Paul and said: "Pack up, Mom, we're in the majors now."

Of course, I had the two kids, so right away I knew this trip was going to be an adventure. If only I knew just *how much* of an adventure.

I had always had either my mother or his mother with me on all the various trips when the kids were little. I always did the driving, but somebody had to hold the baby! Remember, this was years before anybody ever thought of inventing the car seat or even seat belts. And, of course, there wasn't any air conditioning in the cars in those days either. So I loaded up our car to the hilt and then bought this little one-wheel trailer from Sears and loaded it with all our other things, high chairs, potty chairs, baby beds, you name it.

For this trip, Don's mother was with me and we set off on this two-lane highway—there weren't any interstates then—heading east for Brooklyn. When we got about ten miles out of Madison, Wisconsin, I got a flat tire—on the trailer. I was somehow able to control the car and I pulled over to the side of the road, but now I had to get into the city and get help. Remember—no cell phones yet! All I could do was thumb.

As I got out onto the highway, my thumb out hoping to hitch a ride into Madison, my mother-in-law was left standing there on the side of the road in all the heat with Tom, a toddler, and Donna in her arms. She sat in the car for a while but sooner or later it got so hot she had to get out and start walking them around. Meanwhile, finally a tractor trailer stopped. It even had a sign saying "no riders" but the driver, obviously seeing me as a so-called damsel in distress, said: "Ma'am can I help you?"

I said: "Well, as you can see I've got a problem here. The tire on my trailer is flat and I've got to find a Sears to get it replaced or fixed. Do you know if there's one in Madison?"

He said there was and that he'd give me a ride even though he wasn't supposed to, because it was an emergency. It was about three o'clock in the afternoon and I didn't think it would take much time to get into Madison and find the Sears store. So I got into the truck and left my mother-in-law and the kids there with our car and all our stuff. Well, we found the Sears store, all right, but after purchasing two tires, not one (just to be safe), we then had to go to a gas station where I waited until they could free a man up to go back with me to change the tire. By the time I got back, it was six o'clock, and needless to say, my mother-in-law was frantic. She said a police car had passed by every so often but never once stopped and asked if she needed any help. She said if I hadn't gotten back by six o'clock, she was going to flag somebody down and go after me, assuming I'd been kidnapped or something.

What was it Don had said to me? Welcome to the major leagues.

As Buzzie had promised, Don didn't get to play much the rest of that year, but he was assured of a spot on the team for 1955 and that turned out to be one of the great seasons for us when the Dodgers won their first world championship. Even though Don was a backup, the Brooklyn fans treated us like we'd been there forever. Everyone was just so happy that year, and the victory parade through Brooklyn was an experience I'll never forget.

Then came 1956 and, as incredible as it might have been, we found ourselves back in a hospital again with Don the victim of another life-threatening beaning. This time I was watching the Game of the Week on television and saw the whole thing along with everybody across the country. The Dodgers were playing the Reds and Don was given a rare start at shortstop because Walter Alston wanted to give Pee Wee a rest. All of a sudden, as I was watching, Don went down in the dirt after being hit in the cheek (below that protective liner) with a pitch from Hal Jeffcoat. I didn't know where he'd been hit. I was just stunned, in absolute disbelief at what I saw.

After what seemed to be an eternity of everyone hovering over Don as he lay there motionless on the ground, they brought out a stretcher and carried him off the field. All I could think of was how Dr. Lefebvre had said to him: "Don't ever get hit in the head again!" There were soft spots in his skull where they put those buttons after they'd drilled holes to relieve the pressure from the first beaning.

Once I found out they were taking him to Long Island Hospital, I rushed down to my car and drove over there. When I got there, Don was lying on the gurney, still in uniform. His cheekbone had been broken and they feared he might have a detached retina. I remember Gil and Joan Hodges coming in to offer us their support—that meant so much—but for the first time Don was worried. He said to me: "I don't know, Mom. This might be it."

But twenty-four hours later, he was ready to get out of there. The doctors told him they had to repair the cheekbone with an operation in which they essentially popped it back into place like a ping-pong ball.

So the next day, I had to be there real early in the morning for the operation, and Don's sister, Erma, who was a flight attendant for American Airlines, had flown in and was going to go with me. As we pulled up to the hospital, we were trying to find a place to park. There were all these "No parking Saturday and Sunday" signs on one side of the street and "No parking Monday-Wednesday-Friday" on the other side of the street. Finally, on a street where you weren't supposed to park according to the signs, there were a lot of cars parked there anyway, and since I couldn't find a spot, I pulled in there, figuring the worst I could get was a ticket. Twelve hours later, after sitting there all day while Don went through the operation, I went out to get my car and it wasn't there.

As if I wasn't stressed out enough with my husband and now my car was gone! I must have walked around the block three times even though I was sure where I'd left it. I went back into the hospital and the administrator, very apologetically, told me my car had been towed. By this time, I didn't know what to do. I had to get back home where my kids were being cared for by the couple downstairs.

The hospital administrator told me I had to take a cab ride to this lot where the car had been towed. This was 1956, but I still remember: The towing fee was $25 and another $25 for the ticket, and nobody from the Dodgers could do anything about it.

Meanwhile, Don had a long way to go before he was out of the woods. Because his retina was said to be a thread from being detached, the doctors had to fit him with this blindfold so he wouldn't move his eyes. He also was told he couldn't bend down in any way, or tie his shoes or play with his kids for fear the blood would rush to his head. After that, it was another six weeks of wearing these special glasses, also with pinholes in them. He needed round-the-clock care just walking, and his mother came up from Cincinnati and took the kids so I could concentrate everything on him, helping him around the apartment, driving him to all his appointments and for his haircuts and other things.

When Don got the Devil Rays job, which meant we weren't going to have to move anywhere for the summer for the first time in fifty-six years, I sat down and calculated how many miles I'd driven in his career. It came to over a hundred thousand! Probably the most memorable drive—even more so than the St. Paul-to-Brooklyn experience—was when we were in Mobile and I was getting ready to have Tom. My mother had flown down to be with me, but neither she nor Don's mother drove a car. I'd begun having labor pains and when I called the doctor, he told me to get right to the hospital. But when I told my mother we were driving to the hospital, she screamed: "You can't do that!"

Don was coming in off a road trip later that night, and I had told him to go right to the hospital and the car would be there for him to get home. That's why I drove myself. It's funny, though. I keep thinking of today where they've got the nannies and the shipping of the cars and I still think we had a lot more fun with all the hardships. I didn't mind the driving, especially when the kids got a little older and we'd do all the sight seeing on our way to whatever city where Don was playing. When he was in Los Angeles with the Dodgers, we saw the Grand Canyon, the Petrified Forest, and the Painted Desert. The principal of their elementary school always used to let me take them out of school a little early, "The education they'll get doing all that traveling to where their father is playing is much more valuable than the last couple of days in school," she said, and she was right. They loved every minute of it and they got to see things they might never have seen. Once they got into high school, however, it got more complicated when they got into sports and summer jobs.

I have to say I know a whole lot more about U.S. geography than Don, having driven most of the highways in the country. He always jokes about the time Buzzie, who was running the San Diego Padres at the time, offered him a minor league manager's job and he chose Key West because he figured it was close to our home in Treasure Island, next to St. Pete Beach. He had no idea Key West was all the way over on the east coast of Florida and then another three hours south of Miami by car. That summer, 1969, the Key West team made one trip to St. Petersburg for a game and Don called me to say he was bringing the team over for lunch. It was quite a sight, seeing this huge bus pulling up in front of our house with twenty to twenty-five players on it. I cooked a bunch of hamburgers and hot dogs, made salads, and bought soft drinks and we had a grand old time out there in our backyard before they went off to their game.

But this wasn't unusual. Don was great like that. All through his playing days, he would always invite the single guys over for dinner because he knew how much a home-cooked meal meant. My mother always told me: "You should feel complimented by that."

It was always unsettling when Don got traded, but one of the consolations about it was that it usually happened in the off-season when we had time to prepare and find a place to live. But in 1963, after he'd come back to the Dodgers again, we really got blindsided. I was still in Florida and he was waiting for the trading deadline to pass before having me come out to L.A. A couple of days before the deadline, however, he called me and said: "Okay Mom, it looks like it's safe to come out." He'd already gotten an apartment, so I packed everything up in the car and drove cross-country with the kids to L.A. He'd gone on a road trip to the east coast, but I always wanted to get everything settled in our apartments; do the cleaning, washing the windows and screens, and so on.

I'd been there barely a day and I was lying out by the pool, re-laxing, after knocking myself out with all the cleaning—nothing is ever perfect enough for me—when the manager of the apartment complex came up to me and said: "Mrs. Zimmer, is that true what I just heard on the radio? That Don's been traded to the Washington Senators?"

"Are you kidding me?" I said.

I couldn't believe this. I had just gotten settled! I called our dear friend, Buzzie Bavasi, and said: "Is this true? Have you really traded Don to . . . *Washington, D.C.?*"

Don, in the meantime, had flown with the team to Cincinnati and had gone to visit his mom and dad so the team couldn't locate him to tell him. By the time he found out, he called me and I said: "I've already got two bags packed."

On this one, we took our time driving back across the country. We stopped at Don's sister's home in Tulsa and after about a week and a half, we got to Washington where Don had already gotten us another apartment. Thankfully, that was the only time I had to make a move like that in the middle of a season.

The one trip I really regretted making was in 1972 when Don was managing the Padres in San Diego. Tom was already playing minor league ball and Donna was finishing up high school, but that had been one of our longest separations—he'd been a coach there under Preston Gomez and got named manager when they fired Gomez in April. He called and said: "Mom, I need you out here." It wasn't easy driving all the way out there. It wasn't Chicago or some of the other places. I packed up and off I went, but I regretted it because I missed our daughter's high school graduation. From then on, I was always with him, from spring training through the whole season.

I have to say, we had fun every place Don played and managed. There was something about every city that made our stay there memorable. And considering I agreed to get married at home plate, it wasn't like I didn't go into a baseball life with my eyes wide open. I was prepared to live a vagabond existence, probably from the day Don asked me right after that season had ended in Elmira if I wanted to go to Caracas. Through the years, people have asked me if I was just as prepared to live with Don's betting, which is his second life after baseball.

I'm not a gambler myself and there were times way back that I probably worried about the house payments. But he's never been a drinker or a carouser and going to the racetrack is his hobby. It's a form of relaxation for him, and no matter how much he's won or lost at the track, we've always paid our bills. I'm sure he's bet a lot, but I don't begrudge him that enjoyment. Why? Because he's always met his goals, which were to pay his kids' houses off, buy cars for all his grand kids when they turned sixteen, and never have to take out a second mortgage on our house.

I'm sure it probably got a little tight for us early on when Don wasn't making much, but I don't remember ever having a real money crisis. Eventually, though, he just turned his paycheck over to me and I became the financial adviser. The checking account became a problem for him. It was too easy for him to write a check and not tell me about it and then we'd come up short. His problem was that he'd write a check and never bother to subtract it. I told him: "You've got to keep track! Do you think you're just going to remember that?"

I had to take charge of the checkbook, mostly because, in our life, when all these expenses came in, he was gone. I was the one who made the house payments. I was the one who always had to get the car serviced. The kids always managed to get sick when he was on a road trip—the mumps, the measles—and I'd be the one to take them to the doctor and pay those bills. Today, he'll always say: "Mom, I got to go before you because I don't know how to do any-thing," whereas in most marriages it's the opposite. With both our parents, it was the husbands who did everything, from writing the checks to making all the repairs around the house.

People have often asked me what Don is like after a bad loss. I have to say, he's never brought the games home with him. I remem-ber the 1978 Red Sox–Yankee playoff game in Boston. I was sitting in the stands with my friend, Joan Hockridge, who had started com-posing a poem about the Red Sox winning the pennant. As soon as she did that, I had this bad feeling. And then Bucky Dent hit the home run. I know there were stories written later about Don driving all the way down the highway to Florida muttering "Bucky Dent! Bucky Dent!" I don't know if he really did that, but then he might have. We were driving separate cars.

My biggest disappointment was not being with him for his biggest triumph—when the Cubs team he managed won the division title in 1989. They clinched the title on the road in Montreal. I was up in Windham, New Hampshire, with Donna, and they didn't have WGN, the Cubs' station, on their cable. But my son called from Florida where they did have WGN and he gave us a play-by-play over the telephone of all the celebrating going on in the clubhouse in Montreal and the streets of Chicago.

So we went to the playoffs against the Giants in San Francisco and my son, Tom, was a scout for the Giants while Bob Lurie, the owner of the Giants, and Al Rosen, the general manager, were good friends of Don's. Before the first game, Tom was on the field and Mr. Lurie came up to him and said: "It's okay if you want to root for your dad." Tom, of course, had very mixed emotions, but wasn't that one of the classiest things for anyone to say? I still get choked up every time I tell that story, but that was Mr. Lurie.

I guess the most important time I was ever with Don was when he played in Japan in 1966. Other than the winter ball thing in Cuba, he'd never been out of the country and I just felt I should be with him. I didn't take the kids on that one, and I wound up staying three months. Even though neither of us knew any Japanese, we had a lot of fun picking up the culture together. One incident that was not so much fun, however, was when we went to the movie house one night to see a double feature with Norm Larker and his wife. Norm had been Don's teammate with the Dodgers and he had also signed to play a year over there.

When the first movie was over and the lights came on, we saw these huge rats running across the stage. I told Don: "I thought I had felt something hit my foot during the movie, but I didn't want to say anything to you." They were going after the dropped popcorn. What's funny is, Don very seldom goes to the movies and when he does, he usually falls asleep. Yet, when he's home, he'll watch basketball on TV all night, and still get up at 6:30. As a result, he doesn't know too many of the movie stars. Most of the movies he's seen are sports movies. I know he knows Sylvester Stallone because he's seen all the *Rocky* movies, and he knows Kevin Costner, who he met at Yankee Stadium a couple of years ago, from *Field of Dreams*. Other than that, I'm the movie buff and I'll watch American Movie Classics all day. The new movies I want to see, if they're not about sports, I usually have to go by myself or with a friend.

Years ago, when Don was a bench coach in Boston for Butch Hobson, he came home from Fenway Park one day holding a picture in his hand. I asked him: "What's that?"

"Oh," he said, "this old guy, I think he was an actor, asked to have his picture taken with me."

I looked at the picture and burst out laughing. It was Paul Newman!

Naturally, I saved the picture, and that brings up another of my functions as the baseball wife—personal secretary. Going all the way back to Don's high school days, I've kept scrapbooks of his career and I'm up to seventy-five of them now! Every newspaper clip, picture, cartoon, magazine article about him over the last fifty-six years I've saved in these scrapbooks. I used to put in the good and the bad, but nowadays if I see something that upsets me, I don't show it to him and just toss it out. I've been fortunate in that we have so many friends across the country that will send me articles from their newspapers that I don't see. In that regard, I don't think I've missed too many. When celebrities he's met send him pictures or write him letters I always write them back, and through the years, whether Don realized it or not, he was pen pals with a lot of really famous people like Jerry Lewis, Larry Gatlin, and the old bandleader, Harry James.

At our home plate wedding in Elmira, somebody took a lot of pictures—unfortunately in those days there were no video cameras—and we've got a separate album for that. The reception was held in the Mark Twain Hotel in Elmira and after playing in the game the next day, Don went on a road trip. I stayed in Elmira with Janice Roebuck. But I have to say I wouldn't trade our minor league experiences for anything. I know it helped solidify our marriage and I'm proud of the fact that our son is fifty-two years old and has been married for thirty years and our daughter is fifty and has been married for twenty-five years and that we've got four wonderful grandkids. All of this the product of a vagabond life with an absentee father!

I would have hoped the two beanings when he was a young player were the worst of the crises we went through, and while they probably were, there were more to come, especially in his later years as a bench coach. When he was Don Baylor's bench coach in Colorado, we had another real scare as he was stricken with what he thought was a stroke on a bus ride in spring training from Phoenix to Tucson. Fortunately, it happened just outside of Tucson and they were able to get him right into a hospital. I was staying in our apartment in Tucson when I got a call from the team trainer, Dave Cilladi, telling me where they were. I said I'll be right over and Dave said: "No, Don Baylor is coming to pick you up."

I got to the hospital and when I saw him on the gurney in the emergency room, his speech was slurred and he said: "I don't know what's happened."

I waited all night in the emergency room with Dave and Peter Durso, the Rockies' traveling secretary, because, as the doctors explained to me, if Don was going to have another stroke it would be within twenty-four hours. How reassuring! Well, it turned out he hadn't exactly had a stroke but rather what they call a T.I.A., which is the weakening of a vein in the back of the neck. The doctors asked him if he smoked, which he never did, but when he told them he'd been chewing tobacco all his life, they said that was probably the cause; that the juices from that get into the bloodstream faster than cigarettes. He never chewed again.

Then, of course, there was the Chuck Knoblauch incident when Don got bopped in the head once again and became an unintentional celebrity all over again because of that army helmet. I was sitting in the stands for the first game of the Yankees' 1999 Division Series against Texas and all of sudden this foul ball off Knoblauch's bat went flying back into the dugout. I couldn't see what happened, but they didn't resume the game so I assumed somebody in the dugout had been hit by the ball.

"I hope nobody got hurt in there," I said to the person next to me. "I sure hope it isn't my husband."

Well, don't you know, a few minutes later, Allie Torre, Joe's wife, came running over to me and said: "Soot, it's Don!"

My heart sank. All I could think was: "Here we go again. He's been hit in the head by another baseball."

They took me downstairs to the clubhouse and as I waited there, the trainer, Steve Donohue, came out and said for me to come in, but

I knew Don's old-school about women in the clubhouse, so I said: "No, I'll just wait here." He went back inside and then came out again with a message from Don.

"Zim says to go back up to your seat and get a hot dog," Donohue said.

What could I do? He was obviously okay and it was just as obvious he didn't want me coming into the clubhouse to see him. So I went back up to my seat and ordered a hot dog. The next day, after it was in all the papers how he'd been hit again, a fan sent him that army helmet, which he wore in the dugout in the first inning when Knoblauch led off the game.

I can't understand why he's always getting hit in the head. Sometimes I wonder if those metal plugs in his skull are actually magnets for baseballs. In spring training 2004 with the Devil Rays it happened again! He was standing behind the batting cage, too close to the netting I guess, when a foul ball came back and struck him in the forehead, knocking him over. He came home that day with a sheepish grin and gash in his head. Another battle scar!

That was nothing compared to the Pedro Martinez incident the previous fall. This one was all his fault, and after I knew he was okay, I told him I didn't need anymore unnecessary scares like that. Again, I was sitting in the stands at Fenway Park, casually watching the game, when all of a sudden this skirmish broke out. I never saw Don running across the field going for Pedro, the Red Sox pitcher. It was my granddaughter, sitting next to me, who screamed: "Pedro just threw Poppy down on the ground!"

I'm usually calm and collected, but watching him on the ground like that and then escorted off the field, I was in shock. Fortunately, Charlie Wonsowicz's wife, Leslie (Charlie's the Yankees' director of video operations), was sitting behind me and she called her sister, who was watching the game on TV, on a cellphone.

"They're saying on TV he's okay," Leslie assured me. "He's sitting in the dugout with a band aid on his nose."

She'll never know what that did for me. Later, when I went downstairs after the game, Dr. Hershon, the Yankee team physician, told me that Don would have to go to the hospital for tests and X-rays because a person his age could have a broken hip and not know it. At least that trip to the hospital produced some good news. It turned out all he had was a strained groin. Both hips, they said, were in good shape. I do suppose, though, I've got the record for most days in a hospital spent by a baseball wife! We also had the diverticulitis thing in 2003 and when he was playing winter ball in Puerto Rico years ago, he had appendicitis and the organ was close to rupturing. But thank goodness, he's always been a fast healer. The problem is, he forgets he's in his seventies now. I remember him telling me after the second head injury: "I'll never see sixty years old." I'm just thankful I've still got him after all we've been through.

I'm not sure what got into him in running out there after Pedro. I do know they were all under a lot of pressure being that it was the Red Sox and all, and Don was upset over the treatment he'd been given from George Steinbrenner. Before that series even began, he'd made up his mind he was leaving, and he let his feelings be known after they beat the Red Sox. I just didn't want him holding a press conference to announce it after the World Series. I felt that would make him look small.

Those were eight wonderful years we had in New York, the highlights being all the parades down the Canyon of Heroes after they'd won. Those were heady times for us, riding on those floats, the confetti streaming down, and the tens of thousands of screaming fans lined up along the streets. It brought me chills. I know there are parades everywhere for championship teams but nothing compares to New York.

Afterward, we were able to take our grandkids to the mayor's house, Gracie Mansion, for the reception there. The year Don wore the army helmet was especially fun. We were on the first float and there was a policeman every ten feet or so to keep the people from jumping out in front of us. The expressions on the faces of those policemen were priceless as they gave us the thumbs-up. The helmet has become a signature thing with Don.

One of my favorite movies was Jimmy Stewart's *It's a Wonderful Life*. Don, of course, barely remembers seeing it, but that's what we've had—a truly wonderful life. And here I am, fifty-seven years later, wondering what my life would have been if he hadn't said yes to that hayride. It's been some kind of whirlwind!

# CHAPTER
## 10

What's a .235
Hitter Like Me
Doing on the
Letterman Show?

S o I was sitting there on the couch of the TV set of the David Letterman show, and this guy behind the camera with the red light on motioned to me. "We're on the air," he whispered and, as I waited for Letterman to ask me a question, I asked myself one: "What in the hell am I doing here?"

I'm thinking all the way back to my playing days with the Dodgers. Me, the humpty backup shortstop to Pee Wee Reese, sitting there in the clubhouse at Ebbets Field, looking around the room and seeing Pee Wee, Jackie Robinson, Duke Snider, Roy Campanella, Gil Hodges, Carl Furillo, Carl Erskine, and Don Newcombe—to mention just a few—all slowly putting on their uniforms just like me. How did I ever get in *that* company? I don't know how many people have said to me through the years, many of them even my friends: "What is it with you, anyway? How is it that all these famous people, far more accomplished than you, treat you like your actually *one of them*?

I've often thought about this and all I can say is, it's simply one of life's great mysteries to me. I've met and befriended a lot of showbiz people through the years, people like Don Rickles, who's thoroughly skewered me whenever I've attended one of his shows. (Now people all tell me we look alike, which is the best revenge I could ever ask for with him). Or George Clooney, who I met a couple of years ago at Derby Lane in St. Pete where he was shooting a scene from his movie *Ocean's Eleven*. It turned out, he was from Cincinnati and his aunt and I went to the same Western Hills high school.

I meet these people and it's suddenly as if I've known them all my life. I know nothing about movies or politics, and I still can't imagine why anyone would want to put a broken-down old humpty ballplayer like me in a TV commercial. Like Don Larsen, of all people, being the only man to pitch a perfect game in a World Series; or the U.S. hockey team winning the gold medal over the Russians at the 1980 Olympics; or an immigrant Austrian bodybuilder-turned-actor, Arnold Schwarzenegger, winding up as governor of California. Sometimes you simply can't explain things. They just are.

I'll be honest, I usually don't stay up that late, unless I'm watching a baseball or basketball game, so I had only a very casual knowledge of David Letterman when Rick Cerrone, the Yankees' public relations director, came to me in spring training of 1997 and asked me if I'd be willing to do an interview with Biff Henderson, Letterman's assistant.

"Who's he?" I asked.

"He's David Letterman's guy," Cerrone replied. "You've seen him. He's going around the training camps doing a lot of offbeat stuff. He asked for you."

"Why me?" I asked.

"I don't know," Cerrone said, "maybe because he thinks you'll be funny."

Well, I forget exactly what the bit was I did with Biff, but I guess it was what they wanted. We hit it off right away and later on, Letterman had me on the show itself. Aside from all his joking around, I think he's a baseball fan and, in any case, I had a lot of fun doing the interview with him. Every so often now, I'll get a note from Biff just asking me how I'm doing, and when Letterman had his heart operation I sent him a get-well card.

I've just always been comfortable being around celebrities, maybe because, at least with me, they've been regular people. It's funny, but when I've been in the company of famous entertainers or even presidents and big-time politicians, they don't want to talk about themselves or their jobs. They want to talk about baseball. That's so even with fellow sports figures. Baseball is what seems to stir people's juices. I remember during the 2003 season, I happened to be out at Belmont Park and I was sitting in a private box in the clubhouse with Richard Dutrow, one of the trainers. Around the second race, Bill Parcells, who has proven himself to be about the best football coach around, came over with his pal, the talk radio broadcaster, Mike Francessa. Parcells saw me and stopped to say something, and then he came back a little later and we started talking about baseball.

I couldn't believe how knowledgeable he was, especially about baseball in the 1950s when I was playing. He asked me question after question about all the old Dodgers and Giants and before we knew it, we had stayed a half hour after the races were over. This was right before he got the Dallas Cowboys job, and I sent him a letter when he turned that team around like all the others he's coached. Knowing his appreciation for baseball history, I probably should have said something like Durocher or Charlie Dressen couldn't have done it any better.

I know Parcells is close friends with Bobby Knight, and he's another coach for whom I have only the highest regard. I first met Bobby back in the 1980s at a celebrity golf tournament in Idaho, named for Danny Thompson, the Minnesota Twins shortstop who died of cancer in the prime of his career. This was one time, however, when I asked all the questions and did all the listening. We must have talked for over an hour, Knight telling me story after story about motivating players and his coaching techniques. I know what kind of a reputation he has for throwing chairs and getting into beefs with school officials, but in my opinion Bobby Knight is one of the most honorable people I've ever met in sports. The stuff you don't hear about with him is how many of his kids finish school. I know if I had two sons playing basketball, the only coach I'd want 'em to play for is Bobby Knight. They'd either grow up quick or melt.

Both Knight and Parcells got their start in coaching at West Point and I have to believe there's something to be said about that. With each of them, their signature is discipline. I didn't have the opportunity to get any military training. I had wanted to go into the Marines

when I got drafted after high school, but Soot got pregnant and, because of that, I was reclassified 3-A. About the closest I ever got to
the military was when Roger Clemens arranged for Joe Torre, me
and a half a dozen other Yankee people to go to the Pentagon after
the September 11 attacks. I remember as we were sitting in this dining room where they were about to serve lunch, all of a sudden one
of the Marine guards shouted: "Atten*tion!*" I looked behind me and
into the room walks Donald Rumsfeld, the secretary of defense.
Everybody stiffened up. We all got on line to introduce ourselves to
him, but when I got up to him, he said: "Oh, I know who you are! I
know you from Chicago!" Apparently, he lived in Chicago when I
was managing there.

It's really something about the Cubs and their fans. I don't know
if it has to do with WGN, the super station that carries their games
all over the country, or whether it's just because they're one of baseball's oldest teams with a tradition that goes all the way back to
Tinker-to-Evers-to-Chance. I only know I'm forever running into
Cubs fans. One of the biggest Cubs fans I ever knew was Jerry
Lewis. I'm not sure why he was, but we became pals when I was the
manager there. I'd actually met him years earlier in Los Angeles
when I was playing with the Dodgers. Lewis had always wanted to
be a ballplayer, and he'd gotten to know a few of the guys on the
team.

One year, Gil Hodges brought him to the ballpark and gave him a
first baseman's mitt and let him take infield with us. From there, he
started playing in our pepper games and that's where he took a liking to me. When I got traded over to the Cubs, Lewis showed up in
their spring training camp in Mesa, Arizona, for a couple of days,
and after working out with us, he'd go to the dog track with me.

Everybody, of course, recognized him at the track and he'd go into his act where he'd take one hundred or so losing tickets and throw them up in the air and slap me across my cheek. One time, he just threw all the tickets in my face and everybody laughed.

Then, a few years later, a couple of friends of mine from St. Pete went to Vegas with me. We were staying at the Desert Inn, one of the few hotels that had a golf course nearby. As we were walking off the eighteenth hole, here came Jerry, just beginning to play his round. He saw me and threw his arms around me and said: "Where are you going?" I told him we were going to hail a cab to go back to our hotel. "No way you are," he said. "I'm driving you back." And that's what he did, putting off his round of golf.

Now, moving ahead another twenty years, I was managing the Cubs, and Jerry would come through Mesa every spring on his way to or from L.A. He'd spend a couple of days with me at camp and, again, we'd go to the track together. One year, I gave him a Cubs jacket, which absolutely thrilled him, and all through my term as manager there, he'd write me letters, faithfully predicting the pennant every year for us. At the beginning of the 1988 season, he wrote me a letter with my picture attached in the upper right-hand corner. "I want you know," he wrote, "I have blown this picture up to sixty by ninety and it's hanging in my living room so when I feel depressed, I see it, and feel better!"

Soot saved all the letters I got from Jerry, as well as the hundred or so others I've gotten through the years from celebrities. I guess the one I cherish most is the get-well note I got from President Clinton when I was in the hospital in Tucson after suffering my T.I.A. when I was bench coach with the Rockies. I later got to meet Clinton in person when the Yankees were invited to the White House after winning the world championship. As I recall, isn't his wife a Cubs fan too? Or so she says?

We got invited back to the White House again in 2001 after beating the Mets in the World Series—this time by President Bush—and him I got to know him a little bit. Of course, we already had a little something in common in that Bush is a baseball man. Before he got into politics, he owned the Texas Rangers. He and a group of his investors bought the team from Eddie Chiles, the eccentric old oilman who fired me as manager, and I later on kidded him about how close our paths came to crossing. "You got there a little too late to save me," I said.

On that visit to the White House, I had brought along a copy of my book, which had just been published, in hopes of giving it to the president. While we were in the Rose Garden, I approached one of the Secret Service men and asked: "Is there any way you could get this to President Bush?"

He hemmed and hawed, but finally let me take it into the oval office where the president was greeting us. After Bush and I shook hands and said a few words to each other, I showed him the book and he said: "Just put it right there on the desk and I'll get to it later."

The next year he came to Yankee Stadium to throw out the first ball at the World Series, right after September 11. He got there early and was playing catch to get loose, downstairs in the corridor by the Yankee clubhouse. With that flack jacket on, he didn't want to embarrass himself. I was sitting in the dugout while this was going on when suddenly a Secret Service man came up to me and said "The president wants to see you inside." So I jumped up and followed him down the runway to the corridor where Bush was waiting.

"I've been a little busy lately," Bush said, "but I just wanted you to know, yours is the only book I've had time to read."

The one other president I got to know fairly well was Gerald Ford, who was always a guest at the Tucson Open golf tournament, which Joe Garagiola ran. The first year Garagiola invited me, he came around in a golf cart just as I was about to tee off and he said: "I have a private party every year and you and President Ford are invited. I said to myself: "Well, if that ain't something!"

Joe hadn't mentioned anything about the attire and I hadn't brought a tie with me anyway, so I showed up at this party in a sports shirt and slacks. Well, for one thing, this "private" party turned out to be a banquet with about 150 of Joe's most intimate friends and as I sat on the dais, I saw everybody coming in and they were all wearing ties.

Then Joe stepped to the microphone to perform his emcee duties and started going into his shtick.

"I see Zim got all dressed up for the president, didn't he?" he said, and, naturally everybody laughed, especially Ford.

So the next year, when Joe invited me back, this time Soot made sure I didn't embarrass myself again. She packed not one but *two* ties, just in case I lost one or spilled gravy on it. And, once again, Garagiola invites me to the "private little dinner" with President Ford. But as I took my place on the dais again, Ford came into the room and wearing an open-neck sports shirt. When it was his turn to get up and speak, he said: "Just so you folks all know, I wanted Zim to feel comfortable this year which is the reason I didn't wear a tie!"

On the other side of the spectrum from the presidents, I'd have to say my strangest encounter with a celebrity was the one with Ann Landers, the advice columnist. My wife always read Ann Landers in our local paper, but I had never heard of her until the day we got a phone call from one of her assistants asking if I would be kind enough to respond to an angry letter she'd received. It seemed the reader was upset about ballplayers chewing tobacco and doing all that spitting that goes with it.

"If it's against the law to spit on the sidewalk, why is it okay to spit on TV in front of millions of people?" It was signed: "Gagging in Glendale."

The reason Ann Landers chose me to answer the letter was because, at that time, I was probably what you would call a poster boy for tobacco chewing. Me and Nellie Fox of the Chicago White Sox. From the time I played high school ball, as soon as I'd get to the park, I'd grab my bag of Red Man and stick a chaw in the left side of my cheek. I never switched it. Fox always had his chaw on the right side, and one time an AP photographer took a picture of the two of us in spring training, matching chaws. Even though this was long before I had my scare in Arizona that prompted me to give up chewing tobacco for good, Soot thought it was a good idea if I obliged Ann Landers by replying to "Gagging in Glendale." So, with Soot's help, this is what I wrote:

"Dear Gagging: I agree it's a nasty habit and I would not advocate that any youngster take up chewing tobacco or snuff. But chewing does cause excessive saliva. You cannot swallow tobacco juice, and here's where spitting comes into the picture. Players and coaches in the dugout often eat sunflower seeds and they spit out the shells, which may just *look* like they're spitting. Also, I can tell you that a great many more players chew gum than tobacco. I should also tell you that the majority of players who are seen spitting on TV have no idea the camera is on them. Thanks for giving me the chance to bring the facts to the public. Sincerely, Don Zimmer."

Okay, I know it was a cop-out. I'm sure "Gagging in Glendale" wasn't real satisfied with my reply. But if he or she is still out there, I will say this: Chewing tobacco is not only a dirty habit, it's a life-threatening one. I was lucky in that I was given a warning that made me quit. Nellie Fox was not so lucky. He died a terribly painful death from lymph node and skin cancer at just forty-seven years old. I have no doubt it was the result of all that chewing he did. Another big chewer from my generation, Bill Tuttle, the Tigers and Athletics center fielder in the 1950s, died a horrible death from cancer as surgeons kept cutting out pieces of his jaw, the result of the chewing tobacco, until they couldn't stop the spread any longer.

Still on the subject of chewing, long before I quit, I had a little session with Larry Gatlin of the Gatlin Brothers country and western singing group. I'm not really into country music, but this was 1983, when I was a coach for Billy Martin with the Yankees, and the Gatlin Brothers were at Yankee Stadium to perform the National Anthem. Larry Gatlin introduced himself to me and then asked me if I could show him how to chew. We had a lot of fun, and I got a laugh watching him trying to keep from swallowing the juice. A couple of weeks later, he sent me a letter in which he said: "I've been working on my chewing and I've got it all the way up to two minutes before I have to quit. Where in the hell do you put that stuff?"

As I was saying before, it's amazing how so many celebrities are big baseball fans and look to *us* as the celebrities. I can't help but find that amusing. Over the years, quite a few Hollywood stars have gotten involved in baseball. Bing Crosby once owned part of the Pittsburgh Pirates at the same time Bob Hope had a small piece of the Cleveland Indians. When baseball awarded an expansion franchise to Seattle in 1977, one of the Mariners' principal owners was Danny Kaye.

I had gotten to know Kaye before he bought the Mariners—he was another one of the stars who would come around the Dodger clubhouse when we moved out to L.A.—and when I was managing the Red Sox and Rangers and we'd come into Seattle, he would always come down to the clubhouse to look me up. He was just a tremendous guy, down to earth as you could be. It was the same thing with Gene Autry, who owned the Angels from their acceptance into the American League in 1961 until his death in 1998.

"The Cowboy," as we called him, was the nicest, most generous man to ever come through baseball. I remember one of the last times I saw him, I was with the Yankees in Anaheim and we were getting on the bus after the last game of a series there against the Angels. Somebody called to my attention that Gene was hobbling down the corridor on his cane, waving to me. He'd gone out of his way, walking all that way from his private box, just to say hello to me. You think that wasn't a thrill?

Being with the Yankees those eight seasons when we were going to the World Series practically every year, I got exposure like with no other team in baseball. Every day, it seemed, there'd be a different celebrity sitting in the dugout before games, and advertising agencies were always seeking out the Yankees to pitch their products. I can only imagine how much A-Rod is going to make in endorsements now that he's in New York and no longer in Texas. It's so crazy in New York that even I got asked to do commercials there.

I've got to admit, however, I had some serious reservations about the first commercial proposition that was brought to me by Maury Gostfrand, who's Joe Torre's agent at RLR Associates.

"I've got a terrific commercial deal for you, Zim," Maury said.

"What is it?" I asked.

"Oh, you'll love it," Maury answered.

"What is it?" I repeated.

"Hemorrhoids," Maury replied.

*"Hemorrhoids?"* I said. "What am I supposed say about *them?"*

"That you found a way of relief from them," Maury said. "They'll give you the script."

My first reaction was that I didn't want to promote something that I didn't use. But then I remembered, the product I was supposed pitch, Preparation H, was something I had used once many years ago. I was thirty-six years old, at the end of my career with the Washington Senators, and Gil Hodges, my manager, had sent me to Florida to learn how to catch. I wasn't used to all that bending and squatting and it caused an irritation on my behind and, at the trainer's suggestion, I used Preparation H to relieve the pain. So I *had* used it, and that made me feel a little more comfortable about doing the commercial.

Anyway, they set up this commercial shoot at the ballpark in Staten Island where the Yankees' New York-Penn League rookie team plays. I was living in Westchester and I thought that was like going across the street. They sent a limo for me and it must have taken an hour and a half to get there, through New Jersey and over all these bridges, with the driver taking all these side streets. Once we finally did get there, I put on my uniform and waited in the dugout for somebody to tell me what I was supposed to do.

"Just sit there facing the camera," the guy said to me, "and then we want you to start squirming."

The whole bit was that I was to squirm as if to show that my hemorrhoids were acting up, and then get up and walk into the clubhouse only to reemerge with a big smile of relief on my face. Well, we did this in one take and the cameraman said: "Great shot!" and I said to myself: "This is easy. I'll be out of here and back home in no time."

Three hours later, I was still squirming. I said to the guy: "Two and a half hours ago, you said my take was very good. When I came here, my ass didn't hurt. Well, now, believe me, it *does* hurt!"

The only other time I'd done commercials like that was when I was managing the Cubs and I wound up pitching both Popeye's Chicken and Nutri-System with the ads being aired simultaneously. My pal John Vukovich, who coaches for the Phillies, said to me: "You're the only guy in history to get paid to both eat and lose weight at the same time." Every city I went into on the road that year had Nutri-System products waiting for me in my hotel room, and I did lose weight. But I admit that's one thing I've never been too good at.

And even though I'm not too proud of running after Pedro Martinez in the 2003 ALCS and getting myself tossed to the ground like a rubber doll, it did manage to get me to the Super Bowl. Who'd have thought it? A lifetime .235 hitter doing a Super Bowl commercial? But that's what happened when Maury approached me again after the 2003 season and asked me if I'd be interested in doing a commercial for H&R Block that was scheduled to be aired during the Super Bowl.

"That's pretty big," I said to Maury.

"You bet it is," he said, "and you'll be doing it with Willie Nelson."

Well, Willie Nelson is somebody I definitely *did* know, having met him a number of times through the years through Rick Sutcliffe on the Cubs and Goose Gossage, when I was a coach with the Yankees in 1983. Both Sutcliffe and Gossage were huge Willie Nelson fans and went to his concerts whenever they could. But I couldn't for the life of me figure out how America's most famous country and western singer and an out-of-work baseball bench coach could be teamed up in a commercial for tax accountants.

This time, the commercial was being shot in a minor league ball-park in Lancaster, California. I reported out there about a month before the Super Bowl, and was told to just sit up in the stands until they called me. As I'm sitting there in the stands, they've got all these stunt men down on the field kicking the hell out of each other. This must have gone on for a couple of hours and I'm saying to myself: "Whatever they're paying these guys, it can't be enough." It was fascinating, knowing they'd have to cut all this down to thirty seconds.

Finally, it was my turn to do my thing, which was to just sit there in the dugout, holding this Willie Nelson doll, and utter one line to Willie Nelson: "You want me to give this guy a shellacking?" It was really pretty silly, but as I said, I suppose it was on the heels of the Pedro brawl. And now I can say: "What's a lifetime .235 hitter doing with an AFTRA card?"

Another off-shoot, if you will, of the Pedro brawl was this group of Yankee fans from New Jersey who apparently set up a Web site on the Internet to raise money to pay my $5,000 fine for my misconduct on the field. When somebody told me about this, and the fact that they'd already raised $1,900, I was flabbergasted. I don't even know what a Web site is. Neither my wife nor I have ever used a computer. I asked my grandson, Beau, who's a television newsman in Louisville, to find the site and tell them to give whatever money they raised to charity.

Once I left New York, I figured I'd done my last TV commercial

when, just prior to spring training 2004, Rick Vaughn, the public relations VP of the Devil Rays, said to me: "The ballclub is doing a series of six thirty-second promotional commercials and we want you
to be in one of them." I wasn't sure exactly what the commercial
was, even as I was doing it, but it sure was a lot of fun.

In it, they had Tino Martinez, a Tampa native who, like me, had
been brought home by the Devil Rays for the 2004 season, standing
at a street corner as this big stretch limousine pulls up. The back
seat window goes down and inside is a guy wearing a turtleneck
who is obviously supposed to be Steinbrenner. You can hear him
berating and then firing the driver for getting lost, as the limo pulls
up. Then Tino gives him directions to Tropicana Field, adding:
"This is *my* town." As the limo starts to pull away, the driver's window now goes down, and there I am, winking at Tino as I drive off.
When they finally explained to me what it was, I had to admit it
was pretty clever, although I kind of doubt if Steinbrenner thought
it was.

One of the great nights of my life was spent with another
celebrity I'd never met previously but who turned out to be one of
the nicest, most down-to-earth people you could ever know—Paul
Anka. It was about a month after the September 11 attacks and Joe,
his brother Frank, my pal from Tampa Bay Downs, John the Mailman, and I were all out in Las Vegas. Frank Torre's wife, Susan,
works at the MGM Grand where we were staying and she arranged
for us to see Anka's show. They put us at a table right up front with
all the big shots and, on that night anyway, Anka put on one of his
extra shows in which he sang a lot of very touching songs about pa-
triotism and September 11. The ovations just wouldn't stop, and I
know I don't usually get too worked up about anything at concerts

(a lot of times I just fall asleep, which exasperates Soot), but I was moved to tears. It was an incredible show.

After Anka's final number, Susan turned to us and said: "Don't leave. We're all going back to his dressing room."

Well, we went back there and Anka had changed into a pair of jeans and a tee-shirt. There was a table in the middle of the room with a huge bowl of fruit and cheese on it and he told us to help ourselves and offered us a drink. We all sat down and before we could get into telling him how great his show was, Anka started asking us baseball questions. We shot the bull about baseball for nearly an hour when, finally, Anka jumped up and said: "Okay, let's get on to what we all came here for! Let's get to the tables!" With that, we followed him down to the casino and played blackjack the rest of the night. I could see Anka got as big a kick out of being with us as we did with him. I should say right here, I never saw a better show, or met a better guy.

As you can see, being around Joe Torre, you constantly find yourself in the company of big-time entertainers. Joe seems to know them all, from Milton Berle, who was one of his closest friends, to Billy Crystal, who almost became an honorary coach with us as a regular member of our traveling party during all the playoffs and World Series. And, of course, Joe also has all his restaurants where he's treated like the celebrity. But in my eight-year stay in New York, I got to have my restaurant, too, a place called Nino's, on First Avenue between 72nd and 73rd Streets. I say this only because when you come into this place, the first thing that meets your eyes is this huge mural, stretching the entire wall across the waiting area from the bar, in which an artist has painted all these celebrities eating dinner together on a "typical" night at Nino's. There's the Clintons, Donald Trump, Stevie Wonder, Governor George Pataki, Rudy Giuliani, Wayne Gretsky, Barbara Walters, Regis Philbin and his wife, The Sopranos, Joe Torre, Mel Stottlemyre, Yogi Berra, and right in the middle of it all, Soot and me.

So what's a lifetime .235 hitter doing on the wall of a posh New York restaurant? Well, like so many other things that have happened to me, I got to know Nino entirely by chance. During the 1996 season I'd been out to the racetrack with a couple of friends of mine and we came back into Manhattan to get some dinner. One of them knew about Nino's and we walked into the place and right away really liked it. Nino came over to the table and gave us red carpet service with big platters of complimentary fruit and antipasto, while wanting to talk all about baseball to the point where he seemed to ignore all his other customers just to be with us. But he was a huge fan—just how huge a fan I didn't realize until a couple of months later when we got to the World Series.

Of all the championships we won in New York over those eight years I was there, the first one was always the most special to me, if only because I'd found out, to my amazement, Joe had never been to a World Series in his career and the Yankees hadn't been to one since 1981. So you can imagine how electric the city was that fall of 1996, no more so than at Nino's. But when we lost the first two games of the Series against the Braves, I'm sure there were a lot of people who thought the wonderful ride was finally over. Steinbrenner did, I know that.

Not so, however, for Nino Selimaj. We had gone down to Atlanta to play games three, four, and five, and after the workout on the off-day, I got a call from Nino who said he had this dream that the Yankees are going to win the next four games.

"I want you to make Joe promise you guys won't do anything different to upset this!" he said frantically. I said to myself: "This guy is nuts!" But Nino insisted this dream of his was real, so real that he was trying to get a bet down in Las Vegas. I told him: "I hope you're right, Nino. Joe actually thinks the same thing. But no matter what happens, the day after the Series is over, we're going to have a nice celebration dinner at your restaurant. Joe and Mel and I will all be there. That's a promise."

Well, of course, Nino's "dream" came true, but due to extenuating circumstances, I wasn't able to fulfill my promise to him about the celebration dinner. It seemed the mayor, Rudy Giuliani, had planned a big reception dinner for us at *his* house, Gracie Mansion. I called Nino and told him: "There's one guy I can't say 'no' to when it comes to something like this." He, of course, understood, and we had our celebratory dinner at his place the next night. But from that time on, Nino's became my restaurant in Manhattan. In August of 2001, Soot and I celebrated our fiftieth wedding anniversary with a small, private party there. It was around that time that Nino began asking his favorite customers if they wouldn't mind posing for pictures that he planned to use for an artist to paint this mural on the wall. A few of them, I'm told, declined, saying they weren't sure if they wanted paintings of themselves on a public restaurant wall.

The first time I came in, when the mural had been completed, I was blown away. It looks so real and the artists really captured everyone. Nino told me that the people who all declined have since asked if they can be added to the mural. If so, I know at least one so-called celebrity in the bunch who can easily be replaced. It wouldn't be the first time I've been fired.

As far as "portraits" are concerned, I should probably mention the one I *did* turn down, if only so I can now make a public apology here to another nice person who's quite notable in his own right. It was during one of those World Series in the 1990s and I'm sitting on the bench before the game, watching batting practice, when this guy with a big curling mustache approaches me and says: "I'm doing some sketches here, would you mind if I did one of you?" Well, I don't know who this guy is, so I tell him: "No, I'm not interested." He gave me his card anyway and walked away. That night when I went home, I told Soot the story and showed her the card.

"Oh, Pop," she said. "What's wrong with you? That was LeRoy Neiman! He's only one of the most famous artists in the world!"

I saw Neiman a lot of times around the stadium after that, but he never again bothered to ask me if he could to do a portrait. I guess I kind of insulted him.

A similar thing happened a couple of years later when they'd had some sort of celebrity softball game at the stadium prior to our game. I got out there early, as I always do, and I was sitting in the dugout after the softball game had finished when this cute young girl wearing a Yankee jersey comes up to me and asks me for an autograph. I signed the autograph and then she asked if it would be all right if she had her picture taken with me. I said, "sure." We did the picture, she thanked me, and walked down to the end of the dugout. I thought maybe she was someone's daughter who worked for the club or something. Then, a few minutes later, the players started coming out for batting practice and I looked down the bench and there were Jeter and Posada asking this girl for *her* autograph!

It turned out she was Marisa Tomei and, as Soot once again had to inform me, I had not realized I'd been in the company of an Academy Award–winning actress. I just hope she wasn't insulted, too, that I'd never seen any of her movies, because she was very sweet.

Needless to say, the Yankees, because they're the Yankees, have a lot of celebrity fans. But one in particular whose devotion to the Yankees cannot be questioned is Rudy Giuliani. I don't think there could ever be a bigger Yankee fan than Giuliani. I mean, here was the mayor of New York City, making no bones about the fact that he was rooting for us against the Mets in the Subway Series. When it came to baseball, Giuliani forgot he was a politician and that there was another team in town. I got to know him real well during those eight years, and what I'll never forget was him flying back and forth from New York to Arizona for those World Series games against the Diamondbacks in 2001. It meant that much to him. He was also like an extra coach to us, and I enjoyed being in his company through all those great times. I just hope if he runs for president some day he'll keep me in mind. Knowing him, he'll want to open up a new Department of Baseball.

These are the kinds of things I'm going to miss most about New York. I was never anything more than a little-used support player on those great Brooklyn teams, and when I came back to New York in later years it was as a coach. But I was always treated like royalty by the people of New York, and I know I don't have to work there to still consider it my second home. All I've ever been is a simple baseball man, but it's never ceased to amaze me how so many far more accomplished people I've met in this life wanted to be one too. What a game, this baseball!

# AFTERWORD

"We've Got a Nice Little Team Here, Donny!"

I got the phone call from Vince Naimoli, owner of the Tampa Bay Devil Rays, shortly after the first of the year, inviting me to come over to Tropicana Field for lunch. Naimoli had told me a few weeks earlier he had something in mind for me with the organization. Being that I was out of work, I was naturally interested to hear what he had to say. Although Tropicana Field is less than fifteen minutes from my home in Treasure Island, therefore making the Devil Rays my unofficial "hometown team," it had always been a matter of "so near, yet so far," as I'd been gainfully employed by the Yankees ever since Tampa Bay joined the major leagues in 1998.

When I entered the dining room at the ballpark, Naimoli was waiting there, along with Chuck LaMar, the Devil Rays general manager, and my old pal Lou Piniella, the manager. Like me, Piniella lived in Tampa-St. Pete and we'd run into each other on occasion at the racetrack. As a player with the Yankees, he had long ago earned my respect for his on-field intelligence, fire, and competitive nature when I managed against him with the Rangers and Red Sox. Later, I saw how he brought all those qualities to managing when I coached for him briefly with the Yankees in 1986. In my eight years as Joe Torre's bench coach with the Yankees, I'd always gotten a kick out of watching Lou managing the Seattle Mariners and then, in 2003, his home-team Devil Rays. You always could feel the fire and energy coming from the other team's dugout and regardless of the circumstances, we always knew Lou's teams were going to compete with us.

For the first forty-five minutes or so, the three of us just swapped baseball stories and I began to think to myself, "I wonder why they've asked me over here? Just to talk baseball?" Finally, Lou broke the ice.

"Donnie," he said, "this is what I want you to do for me. I've got a full contingent of coaches, so I don't have a real opening there. But what I do want is for you to come to spring training as a special coach and instructor, in uniform the whole time. Then, when the regular season starts, you'll be in uniform before all of our home games and when the games start, you can sit upstairs either in the suites or with the scouts. The main thing is, I want you on my staff and I want to make use of all your experience and knowledge of the game."

Then Vince cut in. "We'd really like to have you be part of this organization," he said. "We think you can bring a lot to us, both in your baseball knowledge and goodwill. I'd like if you could also occasionally meet with our sponsors, etc., in the sky boxes."

"And as for travel," Lou said, "you can make whatever trips you want. I don't want to put too much on you, but obviously I value having another pair of eyes evaluating what we have here."

When they got done laying out everything, they looked at me for my response. All I could think was, "Where has *this* job been all my life? I'm in uniform all through spring training as essentially a regular part of Lou's staff; I'm paid to be at all the home games where I can sit where I want; I get to make whatever road trips I want; and the whole time I'm *home!* Fifteen minutes from my house!"

Even though I had had some very preliminary talks with Lee Mazzilli about a possible job with him in his new situation as manager of the Orioles, this job was too good to be true. In my fifty-sixth year in baseball, I'd finally made it home.

"Great," said Naimoli, "now we have to get you a title. How does 'senior adviser' sound?"

Whatever they wanted to call me was fine with me. This, I knew, was going to be fun, and after the year I'd just had with all of Steinbrenner's crap, I badly needed some fun. It started from the very first day Lou assembled all the coaches in spring training. Fortunately, I knew a few of his coaches—Lee Elia, Chuck Hernandez, and Tom Foley; and the others, John McLaren, Matt Sinatro, and Billy Hatcher were terrific guys who made me feel comfortable right from the get-go. I have a little saying that Soot had printed up on 8-by-10 pieces of cardboard as a joke for my friends: "If you're early, you're never late." I realize that sounds more like something Yogi would say, not me, but I've always been a stickler for being on time. That's why I'm usually one of the first people to arrive at the ballpark. I like to get dressed and go out and sit by myself in the dugout, waiting for the players to start batting practice. What I didn't realize was that *these guys* get to the ballpark earlier than anyone. During spring training, they'd be there at 6:30 A.M., while I'd be coming in at 7:00 or 7:15.

So one morning, I'm walking into the clubhouse and they're all waiting there to get on me.

Foley says, "Senior adviser . . . I guess that means he can come in anytime he wants!"

I know he's got the big needle out for me so I shoot back, "You think this job is *easy?* The reason I'm late is because I was up all night finishing my evaluation reports on you guys!"

Meanwhile, Piniella went out of his way to help me adjust from the "culture shock" of coming from a team with a $180 million payroll that won 103 games and went to the World Series to a team with a $25 million payroll. Over the winter, LaMar and Piniella had made wholesale changes in the Devil Rays, signing a dozen or so veteran free agents—in particular, first baseman Tino Martinez, outfielder Jose Cruz Jr., second baseman Rey Sanchez, catcher Brook Fordyce, third baseman Geoff Blum and utilitymen Robert Fick and Eduardo Perez—to complement the young core: outfielders Aubrey Huff, Rocco Baldelli, and Carl Crawford, and catcher Toby Hall, who had all been up through their own system and were now starting to come into their own.

"We've got a nice little team here, Donnie," Lou would say to me.

I got a kick out of him calling me "Donnie." Made me feel young again. I could tell, too, that Lou was pleased with all the off-season acquisitions he'd made, especially given the limitations of the Devil Rays' payroll. All spring, we'd be talking about things, and Lou would repeat: "We've got a nice little team here, Donnie," and then I'd hear him use that same phrase in talking to the writers.

At the same time, though, I knew how competitive Lou was, and I also knew his intolerance for losing. If nothing else, he expects his players to play smart. These new players were going to learn quickly about that. In one of the luncheons the team had over the winter, Lou vowed the Devil Rays would not finish last. A couple of weeks later, at another luncheon, he said he expected them to make a run at .500. When people started to call him on that in spring training, he said, "What I need to do is have a few more luncheons and we'll be in the World Series." He laughed when he said it, but I knew those modest goals were in fact *his* goals—and therefore they had better be the players', as well.

This was probably never more evident than in one of the first spring training games when Lou walked out to the mound in the first inning to talk to a struggling Damian Moss, one of the new pitchers who'd been signed as a free agent over the winter.

"I didn't like what I was seeing," Lou said later. "(Moss) had shown great stuff warming up in the bullpen, but when he got to the mound, all of a sudden the plate was moving all over on him. He couldn't throw strikes. He told me he was always a slow starter to which I said, 'I'm not sure if you understand the sense of urgency around here.'"

That's Lou. You never have to guess how he feels about something. In a lot of ways, he couldn't be more different than Joe Torre. Not that Joe didn't have a temper, but he's always restrained while Lou wears his feelings and emotions on his sleeve. I, for one, can relate to that.

One time early in the spring, Lou and I were talking in his office when the phone rang. It was Joe, calling from Tampa. He'd apparently been talking to a friend of his who had a horse tip that day. Lou put me on the phone. "Joe," I said, "we don't bet over here."

Actually, the day before, Sinatro had come into the clubhouse all excited about a horse that he'd been given a tip on. It was a can't-miss, according to Sinatro, but as of this writing it still hasn't crossed the finish line.

After the first few weeks of spring training, Lou confided to me about the adjustment he'd had to make coming home to Tampa Bay, where they'd never done anything but finish last. "I've been a winner all my life," he said, "and I've had to learn how to be patient with these kids."

"I understand," I said. "My first year of managing in the big leagues my team in San Diego lost 104 games. I threw chairs up against the wall. I tore up clubhouses. I knocked over the 'spread' table. Then I got myself together and asked myself, 'Are my players trying as hard as they can?' The answer was yes. So how could I be jumping on these guys like this? After that, I backed off."

Lou said it was very much the same with him in 2003. They thought he was a crazy man in that first spring training with the Devil Rays and people in the organization who didn't know him were worrying that he'd never make it through the season. But as much as he couldn't stand the losing, Lou's outbursts were more than anything about effort and playing smart baseball. As the year went on, we on the other side saw a vastly different Devil Ray team than the ones that had been such doormats those first five seasons. Under Lou, the Devil Rays may have still lost 99 games, but you knew you were in a game with them every day. You could see his players hated losing as much as he did and that they were no longer just accepting it.

I see a lot of Billy Martin in Lou. Billy was a fighter who wouldn't hesitate to get on a player in front of everyone else if he felt that player had made a mental mistake. Billy was especially hard on catchers, as Lou is. We had a situation in spring training 2004 when, with two out in the ninth inning and us winning by one run, our pitcher, the right-hander Jorge Sosa, gave up a home run to the White Sox third baseman, Jose Valentin, who was hitting left-handed. In that situation, the one thing on the catcher's mind has to be not to let the pitcher throw the ball over the middle of the plate where the hitter can turn on it and hit over the right field fence. After the inning was over, Lou went right up to Robert Fick, who was getting a rare catching stint that day, and asked, "Where did you want that fastball?"

"Away," Fick said, which was the right answer. It was the pitcher's job to throw it away. Lou will challenge his pitchers and his catchers in situations like that and they better have the right answers. But these are the little things between winning and losing, and that's why Lou is so obsessed about playing smart baseball. Lou is not going to change his personality or keep anything inside. There's no right or wrong way to do things in baseball, but he's very well respected throughout the game for doing it his way.

As I went around spring training with the Devil Rays, I constantly ran into old friends wishing me well in my new job. At the same time, they'd never fail to give me the business about my new title. When we were over in Lakeland one day playing Detroit, I got to see Roger Craig, my old Dodger teammate who was serving as a special spring training pitching instructor for the Tigers.

"What is this *senior adviser* thing?" Roger asked me. "They want you to go up to the suites and talk to the investors and the sponsors? That ought to be good. What the hell are *you* gonna talk to them about? You don't know about anything but baseball!"

I was glad to see nothing has changed with Roger. I was his third base coach in 1987 when he was manager of the Giants, and I must say we were a couple of real dandies working together. Watching us flashing signs back and forth, people thought we were both crazy. We had our own little signals because in Candlestick Park the third base coaching box was a long way from the dugout. I'd stand there in the box, looking in for the sign, and Roger would flash "bunt" and I'd shake him off. Now he'd throw up his hands as if to say, "What the hell is going on?" I'd wave back at him as if to suggest he give a different sign. Now he gives me the two-hand wave of disgust as if to say, "Okay, *you* manage the team!" It was all in fun, and we'd go back and forth with each other until we got it right. We really did understand each other—hell, we grew up together in baseball! But sometimes I'd shake him off just to aggravate him. Later, I'd come into the dugout after the inning and yell at him, "You got so many damn signs I'm missing half the game!"

Candlestick Park was so damn cold, with that wind whipping in from the outfield, and I couldn't wait to get in the dugout between innings to get warm. Roger would always be standing there in the corner of the dugout with his foot on the top step, looking like George Washington crossing the Potomac. I'd run in and get a seat down the bench from him right next to the heater. After a few minutes, he'd look over at me and say, "Zim, c'mon over here." Now I've got to get up and leave the heater. So I'd walk over there and ask, "What's up? What do you need?" and Roger would look at me and say, "Nothin'." Beautiful. That was his way of saying I was looking too comfortable over there.

Roger Craig, Joe Torre, Lou Piniella. You couldn't work for three better managers.

One reason for Lou's "sense of urgency" in spring training was the fact that we had to have our team together a week ahead of everybody else because we were opening the season in Japan—against the Yankees—on March 30. Since I had been to Japan a couple of times before—as a player in 1966 and as a manager of a touring major league all-star team in 1990—I knew a little bit about what to expect. I warned Lou that before every game, these little Japanese gals bow and greet the managers at home plate and present them with a bouquet of flowers. When we arrived back home, a reporter at the St. Pete–Clearwater airport asked Lou if he got any flowers and he replied: "Yeah, I got enough to open up a nursery!"

It was an exhausting trip, made satisfying by the fact that we won the opening game over there. You can imagine how badly we all wanted that. And even though these were now official games, I was allowed to stay in uniform on the bench. That was primarily because the Yankees had brought Yogi, and Joe had gotten permission to have him sit on their bench. Lou said to me, "If Joe can have Yogi, then I'm gonna have you."

After that opening game, which we won 8–3, Lisa Olson, the columnist for the New York *Daily News,* came up to me and asked me my feelings about us beating Joe and my old team. I told her I'd be lying if I said I didn't miss Joe and Mel and Willie Randolph and all the players I'd won with over there. And then, I couldn't resist adding: "But I was pulling for the little Devil Rays. You know, Lisa, we've got a nice little team here."